THE PRESSURE GAUGE MINDSET

A DIY guide to increasing the value of any online business and achieving an exit you can be proud of

BY JAMIE TOYNE

The Pressure Gauge Mindset
Published by Jamie Toyne

Written by Jamie Toyne
Designed & Illustrated by
Zoya Godoroja-Prieckaerts

ISBN 978-0-646-86926-1

AUTHOR FOREWORD

I wrote this book for people who are in the process of selling an online business, planning to sell in the future, or for those of you who are looking to improve the value of your business and therefore your net worth over time. For those of you who are simply curious to know how much the highest bidder on the market is likely to pay for your business today, this book is also for you.

If you feel like none of the above quite apply to you, remember that one thing is for certain: one way or another, you will exit your business at some point in the future. As sure as the sun rises in the East, everyone will exit their business, and you and I are no exception.

For many of you reading this book, your exit is your best chance of a good payday. For those of you who have built businesses from scratch, your exit payday is a chance to recuperate the countless, thankless hours you spent on your business long before there was enough capital to fairly compensate you for your efforts.

For those of you who have bravely acquired an online business with the intention of growing and flipping it in the future, your exit payday is your 'dismount' and will largely determine the success of your investment plan.

Sadly, I've seen far too many entrepreneurs leave a lot of money on the table when they go to exit their business, and many find they can't sell their business at all. Planning ahead and educating yourself on the underlying forces that determine online business value will better inform the way you run your business and ensure you get the payday you deserve when the time comes to sell.

The Pressure Gauge Mindset is a way of seeing your business, as much as it is an approach to running it. The purpose of this book is to teach you how to increase the value of your business and exit on your terms. First you will learn how to use the Pressure Gauge Valuation Model™ to identify what elements of your business are pushing your valuation up and down. Then you will learn how to manipulate these elements to improve the valuation and saleability of your business.

CONTENTS

WHAT WILL THIS GUIDE TEACH ME?

1 How much your business is worth today

You will learn how to accurately calculate the value of your online business using the Earnings Multiplier Method and The Pressure Gauge Model™.

2 How to increase the value of your business

You will learn how the 8 Pressure Gauges influence your Valuation and how they can be manipulated to increase your net worth.

3 How to prepare your business for sale.

You will learn about buyer psychology; how to remove any obstacles in your business that often perturb prospective buyers; as well as how to present your business as an attractive acquisition target.

Before delving in, I want to address some of the burning questions that are on every entrepreneur's mind.

WHY IS IT SO DIFFICULT TO VALUE AN ONLINE BUSINESS?

Lack of publicly available data

Unlike real estate and publicly traded companies, there exists very little comparable sales data that you can access to get an idea of the sale price for businesses similar to your own. This is because most small-to-medium-sized businesses are acquired privately, where everyone involved in the transaction is under a strict non-disclosure agreement. In fact, there is a greater likelihood of you accessing inaccurate information, thanks to fraudulent brokers posting fake sales on their website to attract and prey on inexperienced sellers. Online business Valuation tools can be effective in providing a ballpark range, however the majority of tools skip over many of the questions that buyers will ask, and at the end of the day, *a business is worth what the highest bidder is willing to pay for it*.

Different Valuation methods

There is more than one way to calculate the value of an online business; in fact, there are dozens. While most of these methods produce wildly different values to the ones you are likely to receive on the market, over the course of my career, I've found a couple of legitimate methods that consistently value businesses at amounts close to the final sale price of sold listings recorded. The appropriate method to use will largely depend on the business and the types of buyers likely to be interested. We will explore this further in Chapter 1.3 and 1.4.

Formal vs. Informal Valuations

It is important to make the distinction between a *formal Valuation* - such as a bank evaluating whether or not to grant a loan or line of credit, or a lawyer establishing one's net worth for the purposes of legal proceedings - and an *informal Valuation*, which is not legally binding, but can provide critical insight into your business, its market value, and the changes you can implement to improve your business' value. While formal Valuations are necessary in a legal context, informal Valuations are typically more insightful for getting an accurate idea of how much you can realistically sell your business for today and how you can increase its value over time.

Every business is unique

There are hundreds of interconnected factors that determine a business' value and no business is exactly the same. One may argue that, for example, no two houses are exactly the same, but you can still figure out its value by comparing a similar house on a similar block in the same neighborhood. However, if you apply this same method by grouping five key business characteristics like Business Model, Size, Age, Profit and Owner Time Commitment, you would still be comparing apples with oranges.

Consider two five-year-old eCommerce businesses generating $1 million annual Profit. The first has a positive growth rate of 50% and the second has a negative growth rate of 50%. Which business would you rather buy? How much more would you pay for it? A more granular factor is the risk associated with a business relying on a single source of Traffic to generate Revenue. For instance, an FBA business relying on Amazon for 100% of its sales is generally considered less risky than a content-publishing business relying on a single Traffic source. While they are both characterized by Third-party reliance, the risk for each one is weighted differently.

Every buyer is unique

Just how every business is unique, so is every buyer. Buyers will weigh up the risks and opportunities of acquiring your business with their very own set of scales. Having said that, buyers can be separated into three main profiles - *financial buyers, strategic buyers* and *emotional buyers* - although it is worth noting that buyers can often fit more than one profile.

The Financial Buyer is the most common acquirer of online businesses and is primarily interested in the financial return that can be achieved by acquiring a business. Whether they have any special interest or prior experience in a particular industry is secondary, and thus financial performance Metrics will have a greater impact on the way financial buyers value a business compared with other buyers who may have a strategic angle or an emotional attachment to a particular type of business or market.

The Strategic Buyer typically owns a business that operates in the same or a similar industry and is predominantly focused on capitalizing on the synergies between the two businesses to create long-term value. While financial Metrics have a significant influence on a strategic buyer's Valuation of a business, user Metrics and other factors may have an equal or greater influence. There is no better example than Facebook's $16 billion acquisition of WhatsApp in 2014, where the business had only generated 1.3 million in revenue over the trailing nine months. Facebook didn't value WhatsApp based on financial Metrics, but rather by its user Metrics and its potential synergies with Facebook's Business Model.

The Emotional Buyer is best characterized by the sentimental value they attach to a business.

They typically value online businesses similarly to a financial buyer, however they are often willing to pay a small premium for the right business - especially one they are particularly passionate about. Although business enthusiasts are quick to scorn Investors who make emotional decisions rather than business decisions, some of the most successful business owners I know paid a little extra to outbid competitors and secure a business that inspires them, making the process of scaling their business less exhausting and more fun.

WHY IS MY VALUATION LOWER THAN I EXPECTED?

More often than not, owners expect the valuation of their business to be higher than what the buyers in the market are actually willing to pay for it. Understandably, when someone tells you that your business is worth less than you had hoped, it can feel like a personal affront to the business that you have built. However a Valuation is not to certify all the wonderful effort you have put into building your business. Its purpose is to accurately estimate what the highest bidder in the market is willing to pay for the business *today*.

The two primary reasons that best explain this gap between market value and owner expectation are a *buyer's risk assessment* and an *owner's separation value*.

A buyer's risk assessment is often overlooked and under-estimated by business owners who struggle to fully grasp the risks (or perceived risks) a buyer weighs against the opportunity. If, for whatever reason, the business fails, the buyer's upfront investment is at stake. After all, the buying motive is not only to achieve a high ROI (Return on Investment), but also to minimize the risk of losing money. Unlike owners, buyers don't have the same intimate knowledge of the business, so they usually adjust their Valuation to account for the unknown.

Owner's separation value relates to the personal attachment and sentimental value that is often constructed in the hearts and minds of many entrepreneurs. Unfortunately, the esoteric value one places on their own business does not always line up with the amount that the highest bidder in the market is willing to pay at that moment in time. The purpose of a Valuation is to accurately predict what this amount will be.

Alas, it goes without saying that in order to achieve a successful exit, the market's Valuation and your own need to align.

HOW CAN I SELL MY BUSINESS FOR THE PRICE I WANT?

While it is important to consider how the marketplace will value your business, the value *you* place on your business is equally important. Unless under duress, you don't have to let go of your business for a penny less than you want to. In fact, you can systematically manipulate certain aspects of your business that can align the market's value with your own. I've structured the remainder of this book to equip you with the information needed to accomplish this.

WHAT ON EARTH IS THE PRESSURE GAUGE MINDSET?

The Pressure Gauge Mindset is a way of running the business with an end in mind. The mindset is underpinned by The Pressure Gauge Model™, which measures how internal and external factors boost or hamper the value and saleability of your business. We will look at The Pressure Gauge Model™ in closer detail towards the end of the first chapter, but before we do, we need to grasp the fundamentals of how an online business is valued today.

KEY TAKEAWAYS

INTRODUCTION

- One way or another, you will exit your business at some point in the future.

- For many of you reading this book, your exit will be your best chance of a good payday.

- In this guide, you will learn:
  - How much your business is worth today,
  - How you can increase its value, and
  - How to better prepare it for sale.

- It's difficult to value an online business because:
  - Lack of publicly available data
  - Different Valuation methods
  - Every business is unique
  - Every buyer is unique

- The three main buyer profiles are:
  - **Financial Buyers** are most common and determine their Valuation based on financial Metrics and their expected Return on Investment.
  - **Strategic Buyers** who look to capitalize on synergies between the two companies to create long-term value.
  - **Emotional Buyers** who are best characterized by the sentimental value they attach to a business and the small premium they are willing to pay for a business or market niche they are passionate about.

- If your Valuation is lower than expected:

- Always seek a second and third opinion.

- Don't take it personally, they are not designed to reflect the blood, sweat and tears you have poured into your business, only what the highest bidder is likely to pay for it on the market today.

- It typically means there is a gap between our own *separation value* and a *buyer's risk assessment.*

- You can systematically manipulate certain aspects of your business that will increase its value and align the market's value with your own.

THE FUNDAMENTALS OF VALUING AN ONLINE BUSINESS

1

1. THE FUNDAMENTALS OF VALUING AN ONLINE BUSINESS

Once you fundamentally understand how brokers and buyers will value your business, this knowledge can (and should) inform the way you run your business to increase its value and avoid leaving hard-earned money on the table when the time comes to sell.

1.1 THE BEST WAY TO VALUE AN ONLINE BUSINESS

Although there are many ways you *can* value an online business, the only one I can recommend is the Earnings Multiplier method. One reason it has become the industry standard is because it is the most widely understood and most commonly used method amongst buyers, brokers and valuers across the globe. Another reason is because this method allows people to grasp its logic almost immediately by creating a common language around one simple, universally understood figure:

"How is that business listed at 4.1x when sales are trending down?"

"The most I'd pay for a business like that is 2.6x."

"It wouldn't make any sense for me to sell my business for less than 3.8x."

The scoring is so *easy* - the higher the Earnings Multiplier, the higher the value. The only real gripe some people seem to have with this method is that it's *too simple*. People assume that the formula does not fairly consider the more intangible, esoteric Assets of an online business, such as high search engine rankings, loyal customers and great domain names. However, quite the opposite is true. As you will learn in this book, the Multiplier considers all aspects of a business and despite appearing simple in design, there are hundreds (some would argue thousands) of interconnected factors this formula takes into account. If you are still not 100% convinced, let's delve into why other Valuation methods aren't nearly as accurate.

Discounted Cash Flow Analysis	✗
Earnings Multiplier	✓
Cost-based Approach	✗
Comparable Sales	✗
Pre-money Valuation	✗

1.2 WHY OTHER VALUATION METHODS FALL SHORT

There are many methods you can use to value an online business and each one is likely to spit out a different number. It can be tempting for a business owner to argue that a different method should be used to value their business, especially if the

Earning Multiplier method produces a Valuation that's significantly lower than expected. Disgruntled business owners will say things like:

> *"The domain name is worth $20,000 alone."*

> *"Our business offers a similar product to a business that sold for $25 million."*

> *"The growth potential for my business is huge."*

Eventually, they have to concede that there is little point in using a Valuation method that potential and eventual buyers do not understand or agree with. So, let's explore some other Valuation methods to understand why they often fall short for most small-to-medium-sized online businesses.

1.2.1 COST-BASED APPROACH

Cost-Based Approach, also known as an *Asset-Based* approach, is underpinned by the theory that *Cost equals Value*. If this was exclusively the case, you could light money on fire and receive a higher Valuation for doing so. Most owners understand that using this model is not a good idea. However, some owners can't resist the temptation of compounding value, especially if they feel like the time, money, and effort they have invested in the business are yet to pay off.

This method is most commonly used in conjunction with the Earnings Multiplier Method, where an additional cost-based value will be added to the Earnings Multiplier Valuation. Take the owners of Insurance.com for instance, who purchased the domain name for $35.6 million USD in 2010. If the business was valued at $50 million USD today, one might argue that the domain's value should be added on top of the company's Valuation to total $85.6 million. However, what would the value of the company be without the Insurance.com domain? How would site Traffic and sales be affected if the company switched the website URL to getinsurancetoday.com? One can speculate, but it is impossible to say with any certainty.

Other common temptations include large social media accounts, user databases, email lists, and so on. However, the question will always be, what would the business' value be without these Assets? Does this mean that high-quality Assets have zero influence on a business' Valuation? Absolutely not. If your business has developed or acquired a particular Asset with immense future potential, it would influence the Earnings Multiplier accordingly.

The only legitimate case where a cost-based approach is warranted is where an eCommerce business stocks physical products. Even then, the inventory value is usually valued separately from the company, based on a percentage of the goods' wholesale price. The percentage usually depends on the clearance rate of particular products, usually between 70% to 100% of the wholesale value.

1.2.2 COMPARABLE SALES

Comparable Sales is where you determine a business' value by benchmarking recent sales of similar businesses. Let's say you own a business that sells socks and you find out that a competing sock business has recently been acquired for $500,000.

After conducting some research, you establish that the sock business appears to be a similar size, selling similar products to the same customer base. All considered, it is safe for you to assume that your sock business is worth approximately $500,000 as well, right? Wrong.

More likely than not, you'll be comparing apples to oranges because you have only considered three variables of potentially hundreds, and a single variable can significantly swing the valuation in either direction, or render your business unsellable all together. The only useful application for comparable sales is establishing your Base Multiplier, which is the essential starting point when using the Earnings Multiplier method.

1.2.3 PRE-MONEY VALUATION

Pre-Money Valuation is a term coined to a group of different methods used to value immature businesses (or Startups) that have yet to turn over much Revenue or Profit. This approach is only useful if you are looking to source external investment, thus allowing Investors to determine the value of the Equity they are purchasing in return for their cash investment.

Valuing Traffic and Users is a Pre-Money Valuation that deserves special mention, as it is commonly applied to online businesses. Organic Search Traffic can be valued by establishing the equivalent advertising cost of producing the same number of site visitors for specific search terms. A simple calculation would be to take the Cost Per Click (CPC) Rate of each major search term the site organically ranks for, and multiply it by the number of site visitors each search term has organically generated over the Trailing 12 Months (TTM).

A business can also be valued by its user base. This method essentially places a dollar value placed on each user. This dollar value can be determined by using the Average Revenue Per User (ARPU), in which the total number of Users is divided by the total annual Revenue. This is how Facebook arrived at the astronomical figure of $19 billion when they acquired WhatsApp.

It is entirely possible that you will arrive at an astronomical Valuation using pre-money Valuation methods, and while it is tempting to use a method that spits back the biggest number, it is important to remember that you will need to convince Investors of your Valuation, and one day you will have to deliver on their expectations.

I cannot recommend this method for 99.9999999% of the people reading this book, however if you have a hunch you're sitting on a unicorn business like WhatsApp, put this book down and call me right away.

1.2.4 DISCOUNTED CASH FLOW (DCF) ANALYSIS

Discounted Cash Flow (DCF) Analysis is arguably the most comprehensive business Valuation method out there. However, its application is really only suitable for large companies in a mature stage of their life cycle, whereby Cash Flow can be considered stable and predictable. In other words, a company's intrinsic value is determined by projecting the business' future Cash Flow.

The projected Cash Flow is discounted because the model considers the *time value of money*, which predicates that *a dollar today is worth more than a dollar tomorrow*. The limitation of this model is that its accuracy is entirely dependent on the information you feed it. Most online businesses are either too small, too young, too volatile or simply don't have sufficient financial reporting data to support such a method.

I can only recommend using this approach if your business generates more than $25 million in Revenue, $1M in Profit and has more than 5 years of consistent performance with meticulous financial records available.

1.3 EARNINGS MULTIPLIER

All of the other valuation methods mentioned above use different inputs and will therefore produce different outputs - none of which are likely to paint a realistic picture of what your business *is actually worth*. By now, there should be no doubt left in your mind that the *Earnings Multiplier Method* is the most appropriate method to use when valuing your online business. The formula couldn't be more simple:

Business Earnings x Multiplier = Current Market Value

If a buyer values a business that is currently earning $100,000 a year at "3x" Multiplier, it would be calculated like this:

$100,000 x 3 = $300,000

If the buyer acquires the business for $300,000 and it continues to earn $100,000 a year, the buyer can expect to break even on their investment in three years' time.

	Acquisition	Year 1	Year 2	Year 3
Earnings	$100K	$100K	$100K	$100K
Debt	-$300K	-$200K	- $100K	$0

The Earnings Multiplier Valuation method is predicated on the following assumption: *the more valuable the business is, the more buyers are willing to increase their break-even point*. That is to say - the higher the value, the higher the Multiplier. The relationship between the Multiplier and value is demonstrated in the following graph:

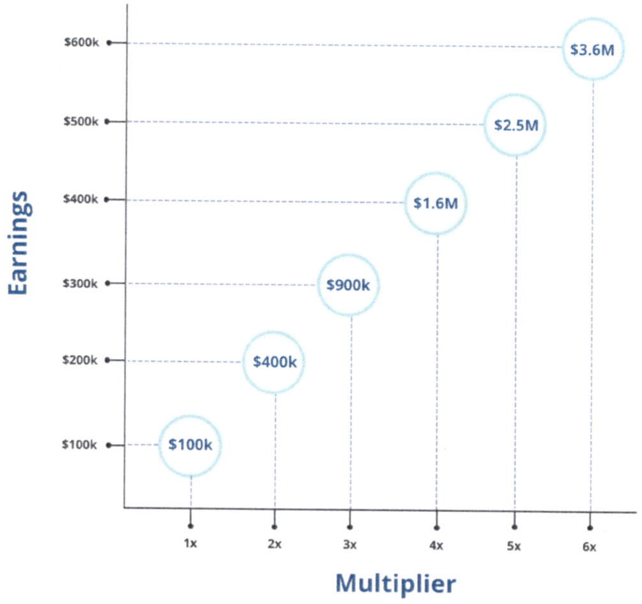

1.4 CALCULATE YOUR EARNINGS

Earnings x Multiplier = Current Market Value

There are two main ways to calculate your

Earnings: Seller's Discretionary Earnings (SDE), and Earnings Before Interest, Taxes, Depreciation, and Amortization (EBITDA). Generally speaking, SDE is best suited for smaller businesses and EBITDA for bigger businesses.

1.4.1 CALCULATING EBITDA

EBITDA = Revenue - Cost of Goods Sold - Expenses + Depreciation + Amortization

If your business is generating more than $15 million per annum, then using EBITDA to calculate your earnings is likely to be the right method to use. Unlike Seller Discretionary Earnings (SDE), owner drawings and other discretionary expenses are not typically 'added back' to the bottom line of a business when using the EBITDA method.

This is because the most likely buyer for a business this size is a corporation or private equity firm rather than an owner-operator like me. If I were to buy your business and operate it, I would consider any income you draw from the business, as well as any discretionary or unnecessary expenses to be potential income I would earn myself from running the business. However, corporations and private equity firms will typically look to employ a director and/or a team to run your business and therefore it won't make sense to add back the wage you draw from the business.

1.4.2 CALCULATING SDE

SDE = Revenue - Cost of Goods Sold - Expenses + Owner Compensation + Unnecessary Costs

This method is more commonly used to calculate Earnings for smaller owner-operated businesses typically generating less than $15 million in Revenue. The critical difference is that owner compensation is *'added back'* to the business's Earnings, meaning that any money the business paid its owners is deducted from the operating Expenses. Owner compensation includes any salary, drawings or dividends received by the owner(s) of the business. It is also common to add back any unrelated, unnecessary or one-time costs that wouldn't necessarily be incurred under new ownership.

So, what is reasonable to add-back, and what is not?

The ambiguous term *'add-backs'* refers to business Expenses which are not critical to generating core Revenue. It is then up to the discretion of the owner, valuer, broker, or prospective buyer to determine which Expenses should, and should not, be subtracted from the operating costs, adding back to the profitability of the business. Ultimately the buyer will determine what the necessary operating costs of the business are likely to be under their ownership. Because *each buyer is unique* and discretionary expenses are essentially a matter of opinion, it is impossible to provide a definitive list that separates *reasonable* from *unreasonable*. However, on the next page are a few examples that will hopefully give you a sense for what I mean.

What if there are multiple owners?

If multiple owners operate the business and their combined weekly efforts amount to more than the standard 40-hour workweek, buyers and valuers will likely consider this when valuing your business. For example, a trio of owners, each one working

Reasonable Add-Backs	Unreasonable Add-Backs
Personal Subscriptions I see all kinds of things on clients' financial statements, and a subscription to Netflix or Audible are by no means one of the stranger ones. If ever questioned by tax authorities, you can claim these are legitimate educational business expenses. However, you could just as easily argue to a buyer that these same expenses are unnecessary personal expenses that should be excluded from the operating cost when valuing your business - and most buyers won't argue with this claim.	**Staff wages & bonuses** It is common for business owners to feel like they could reduce staffing costs without impacting the bottom line. However, any claim to add these costs back would be dismissed by almost any buyer because there's no way to prove this without actually making the changes and monitoring performance for a year or so. An experienced buyer will also know how important human resources are and that remuneration and incentives will need to continue (if not improve) to maintain or grow performance.
Travel (transport & accommodation) Some travel expenses are reasonable to be added back, while others aren't. When you travel to a conference or tradeshow, the flights and accommodation are a necessary expense that should not be added back because you wouldn't have been able to promote your business without being there. However, if you decide to take some clients out for a nice meal, or you extend your stay to explore the city, then you can reasonably claim these additional costs as add-backs.	**Marketing & advertising** Owners may feel like some (or all) of their marketing expenditure is ineffective, and therefore sales performance would not be affected if marketing costs were reduced or eliminated entirely. But again, you can't expect a buyer to take your word for it. You would need to implement the changes and wait 6-12 months to collect enough measurable data that demonstrates that the business can perform just as well with lesser marketing costs.

Note: This table is by no means exhaustive. There are many more examples of reasonable and unreasonable Add-Backs for possible consideration. Keep in mind that Add-Backs are wholly subjective, and just because you consider it appropriate to add back a articular cost, does not mean a valuer or a buyer will necessarily agree with you. Every interested buyer will run their own calculation on the costs of operating the business under their respective ownership and value your business accordingly.

the standard workweek, results in 120 weekly owner hours dedicated to their business. If the eventual acquirer of your business is a sole Owner Operator, they will need to employ more people to maintain performance, adding significant cost to the business. In this case, the buyer would only add back one of the three owner's salaries when calculating SDE.

Calculating Revenue

Despite calculating costs differently, both SDE and EBITDA methods calculate Revenue in exactly the same way. For the most accurate Valuation, I recommend business owners to calculate their Trailing 12 Months of Revenue.

If, say, it is the month of December, 2021, then the Trailing 12 Months would be the months between

EXAMPLE TRAILING 12 MONTHS OF REVENUE

Month	Dec 2020	Jan 2021	Feb 2021	Mar 2021	Apr 2021	May 2021	Jun 2021	Jul 2021	Aug 2021	Sep 2021	Oct 2021	Nov 2021
Earnings	$10,245	$9,754	$10,389	$9,775	$12,456	$10,235	$13,201	$9,661	$9,894	$10,128	$11,459	$13,722

December 1st 2020 and November 30th 2021. You don't typically report the current month you're in because there is little sense in measuring an incomplete months' performance.

1.5 CALCULATE YOUR MULTIPLIER

Earnings x Multiplier = Current Market Value

Let's quickly refresh our memory. We already know that the Multiplier is the number that is multiplied by a business's Earnings to determine its value.

Desirability = Multiplier

We also know that the Multiplier is a measurement of a business' *desirability*. The more desirable the business, the higher the Multiplier score.

That is to say; buyers will pay higher Multiples of Earnings for businesses that are more desirable and lower Multiples of Earnings for businesses that are less desirable. The two primary elements that determine the *desirability* and therefore value of a business can be distilled into *risk vs. opportunity*.

Risk x Opportunity = Desirability = Multiplier = Value

Simple right? Not exactly. Some aspects of risk and opportunity are very subjective, which buyers will calculate differently depending on their individual circumstance. In this guide, bit by bit, you will learn how to minimize risk and maximize opportunity in your business to increase the value of your business.

1.5.1 HOW RISK IMPACTS VALUE

Risk measures the resilience and Sustainability of a business. *What would it take to derail your business? A paperclip or an atomic bomb?* Put simply, Buyers are looking to make a good return on their investment and will determine the likelihood by assessing the innumerable risk possibilities that exist when acquiring and operating someone else's business. This is why businesses with less risk exposure sell for higher Multipliers than businesses with high risk exposure.

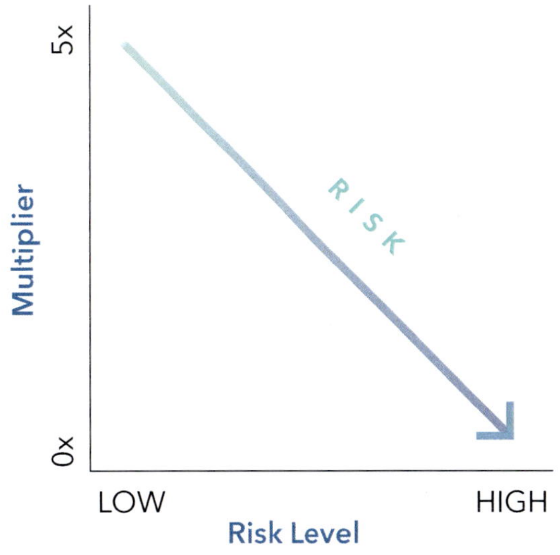

Put simply, Risk creates downward pressure on the Multiplier.

1.5.2 HOW OPPORTUNITY IMPACTS VALUE

Opportunity measures the untapped growth and Scalability of your business. *What would it take to grow your business by 10x? A pocketful of change and some digital marketing activities or a multi-million dollar investment and an entirely new Business Model?* All things equal, businesses with 'low-hanging fruit' will generally receive higher multiples because actualizing growth potential requires minimal effort.

The next diagram demonstrates how Opportunity creates upward pressure on the Multiplier.

Ultimately, risk is the potential for loss and opportunity is the potential for gain. A buyer will weigh up these two elements to determine the value of your online business.

While opportunity is an important consideration when valuing an online business, risk tends to influence the Multiplier much more than opportunity, because the Buyer takes on the risk at the time of the acquisition, whereas the Buyer will have to realize the potential growth opportunity themselves in the future.

1.6 THE PRESSURE GAUGE MODEL™

Now that you fundamentally understand how the majority of online businesses are valued on the market today, it's time to introduce The Pressure Gauge Model™. I have spent the better part of the last decade developing this model with the aim of removing as much mystery from the Earnings Multiplier and thus your valuation, as well as teaching people how to adopt a 'Pressure Gauge Mindset' to increase the valuation and saleability of their business.

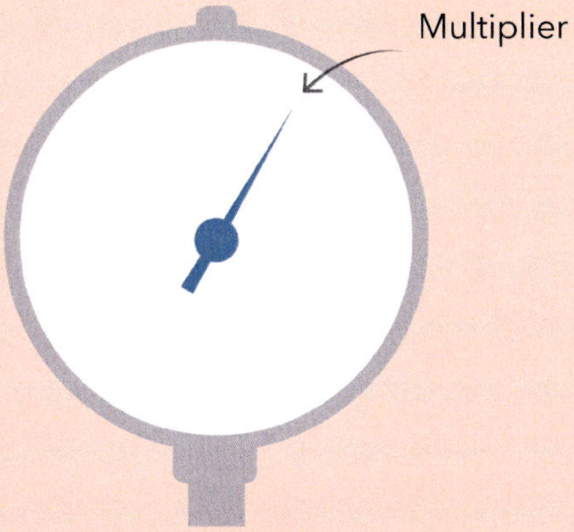

As the name suggests, The Pressure Gauge Model™ measures the pressure applied to your Earnings Multiplier. We already know that Risk creates Downward Pressure and Opportunity creates Upward Pressure on the Multiplier. We also know that it is the intersection of these opposing forces that determine the Earnings Multiplier.

Downwards Pressure moves the needle to the "left" reducing your valuation.

Upwards Pressure moves the needle to the "right"reducing your valuation

The trouble with trying to measure Risk and Opportunity to determine business value is the high degree of subjectivity between individual buyers in the market. These two broad categories don't extract enough quantifiable data for you to effect measurable change in your business. Whereas the Pressure Gauge Model™ performs this exact function, allowing you to accurately measure hundreds of internal and external pressures in a simple and intuitive way.

THE 8 PRESSURE GAUGES

There are eight pressure gauges that measure how different aspects of your business impact value and saleability.

1 Base Multiplier

The starting point or baseline Valuation that is established based on overarching statistics such as Business Model, Business Size, Business Age and Owner Time Commitment.

2 Performance

The overall health of the business and its predicted future Cash Flow based on historical performance Metrics.

3 Sustainability

The likelihood of sustaining a business' performance and ongoing success in the future, based on customer-centric factors and its overall level of resilience towards changing market conditions.

4 Defensibility

The ability to defend market share from existing competitors and new entrants based on a number of internal and external factors.

5 Scalability

The ability to which a company can grow its Revenue while maintaining or reducing its base operating costs.

6 Transferability

The ease to which the tangible and intangible Assets of a business can be transferred from one owner to the other, as well as the level of risk associated with the transition.

7 Auditability

The degree to which key historical performance Metrics, including web Traffic and financials, can be verified.

8 Miscellaneous

The 'catch-all' Pressure Gauge that considers a group of miscellaneous Pressures that aren't always fully captured in the first 7 Pressures Gauges of The Pressure Gauge Model™.

It's important to understand that there are two types of gauges:

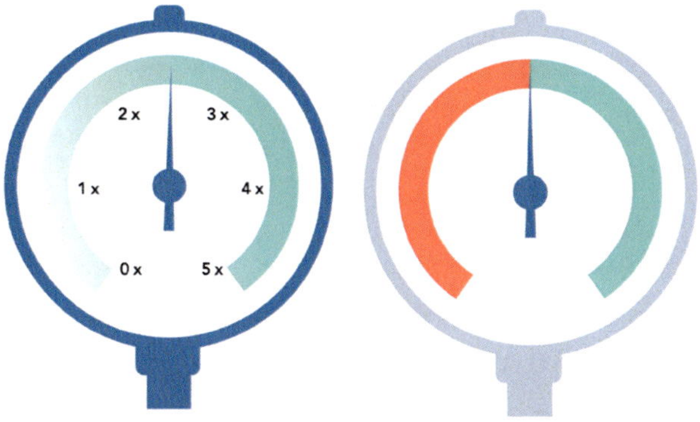

Earnings Multiplier

Pressure Gauges

Some of these Pressure Gauges can create significant pressure in both directions, whereas others can only create significant pressure in only one direction. In the diagram below you can see how the left Gauge measures Auditability, which creates significant Downwards Pressure on your Multiplier if you score low in this area and little Upwards Pressure if you score high. Whereas the Performance Gauge (middle) can have a big impact in both directions and the Scalability Gauge (right) creates much more Upwards Pressure than Downwards Pressure.

Auditability

Performance

Scalability

These eight Pressure Gauges will ultimately determine your Earnings Multiplier and therefore the value of your business. Once you have established your Base Multiplier, the remaining seven Pressures will drive the needle (your Valuation) up or down.

DASHBOARD OF GAUGES

Each Pressure Gauge has its own pressure range. You can see here how each can create Upwards and Downwards pressure on your Earnings Multiplier. Together, the surrounding Pressure Gauges influence your final Earnings Multipler, i.e. your final valuation.

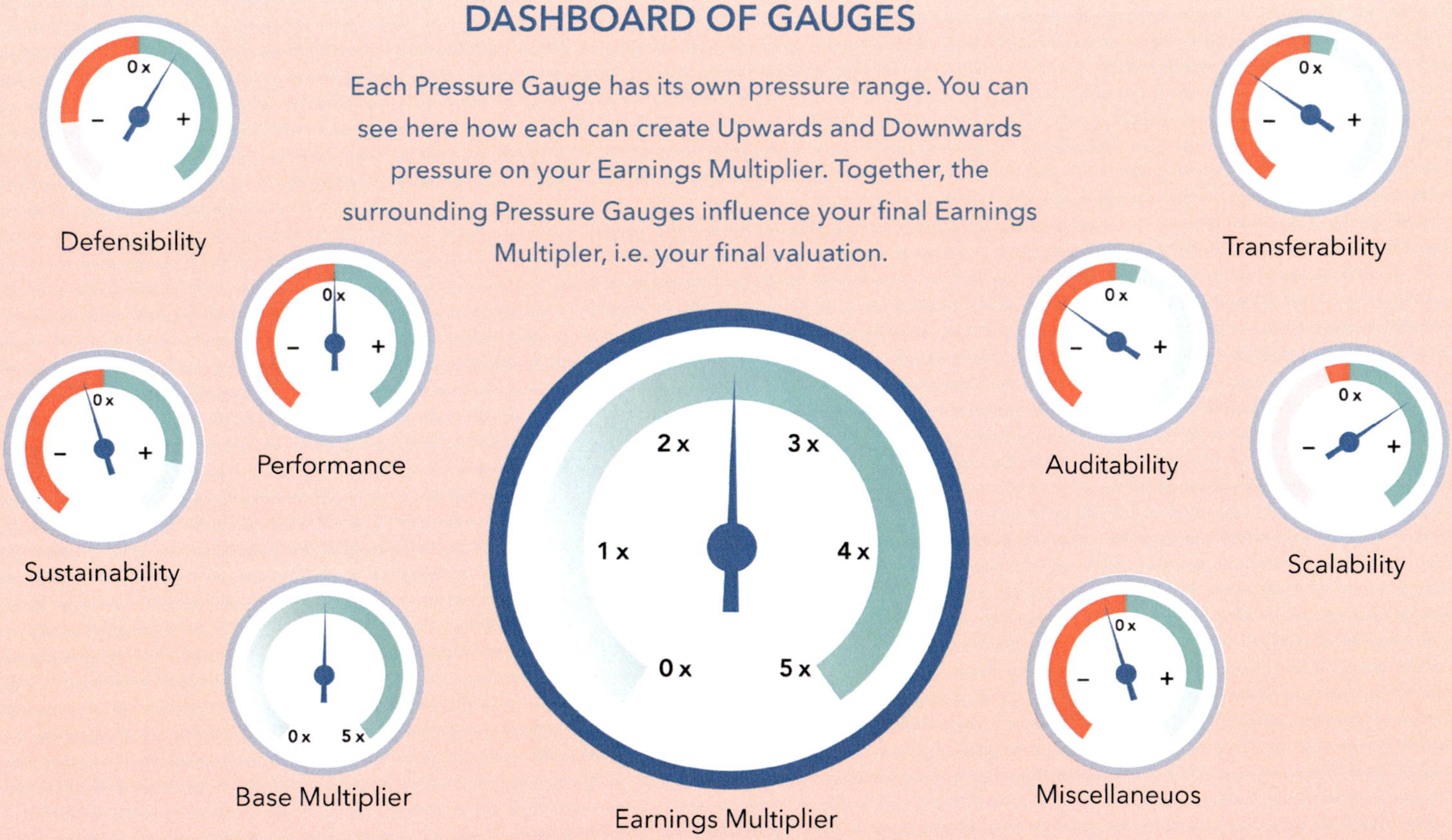

The rest of this book is dedicated to teaching you the Pressure Gauge Model™ and how this mindset will help you to pull the right levers in your business to increase its value and saleability.

ACTIVITY 1

Calculate your Earnings

1. Update your bookkeeping so that all business transactions are properly recorded up to the present month you are in.

2. Create (or download) a Profit & Loss Statement with a month-by-month breakdown of the Trailing Twelve Months (TTM) . *E.g. Month 1 in Column A, Month 2 in Column B, and so on.* See Calculating Revenue above for my info.

3. Select the appropriate Earnings calculation method for your business. If you select the SDE, you will need to create an additional section between the Operating Expenses Total and Net Income called 'Add-Backs'. See example below and refer to 1.4.2 Calculating SDE for detailed instructions.

Meals, Entertainment, Travel	$0	$800	$50
Owner Bonus	$3,000	$1,500	$3,500
Total Expenses	**$18,522**	**$17,505**	**$19,156**
Add-Backs	**Oct-21**	**Nov-21**	**Dec-21**
One-time Expenses	$0	$800	$50
Owner Bonus	$3,000	$1,500	$3,500
Total Add-Backs	**$3,000**	**$2,300**	**$3,550**
Net Income	**$26,228**	**$30,825**	**$32,644**

4. Write down your Trailing Twelve Months Earnings:

____

KEY TAKEAWAYS

THE FUNDAMENTALS

- The best way to value an online business is by using the Earnings Multiplier method.
    - Earnings x Multiplier = Current Market Value

- The Earnings Multiplier Valuation method is predicated on the following assumption: the more valuable the business is, the more buyers are willing to increase their Break-even point.

- When calculating Earnings, use SDE unless your business is generating more than $20 million a year, in which case, use EBITDA.

- EBITDA = Revenue - Cost of Goods Sold - Expenses + Depreciation + Amortization

- SDE = Revenue - Cost of Goods Sold - Expenses + Owner Compensation + Unnecessary Costs.

- When using SDE, it is important to know which operating costs you can add-back and which ones you cannot.

- Reasonable Add-Backs: Personal expenses, insurance, payroll taxes, etc.

- Unreasonable Add-Backs: Staff wages, staff bonuses, marketing costs, etc.

- If multiple owners operate the business and their combined weekly efforts amount to more than the standard 40-hour workweek, buyers will often adjust Owner Drawings accordingly.

- Buyers will weigh up the risk vs. opportunity when determining the value of your business. Risk creates downward pressure on the Multiplier and Opportunity creates upward pressure on the Multiplier.

- Risk tends to have a greater impact on value than Opportunity because the buyer takes on the risk at the time of the acquisition, whereas they must realize the potential growth opportunity themselves in the future.

- The Pressure Gauge Model™ is made up of eight pressure gauges that measure internal and external factors that create Upward Pressure and Downward Pressure on the Earnings Multiplier. The eight pressure gauges are:
    - Base Multiplier
    - Performance
    - Sustainability
    - Defensibility
    - Scalability
    - Transferability
    - Auditability
    - Miscellaneous

GAUGE YOUR BASE MULTIPLIER

2

2. GAUGE YOUR BASE MULTIPLIER

Consciously or unconsciously, Buyers, brokers and independent valuers all begin their Valuation from a starting point to which they base their Valuation on. This is called the *Base Multiplier*.

The Base Multiplier is determined through a process of benchmarking a handful of online business characteristics against historical sales data. The four most common include *Business Model, Business Size, Business Age* and *Owner Time Commitment*.

Although it would be foolish to value a business on comparable sales alone, I recommend using market averages to establish a ballpark Base Multiplier.

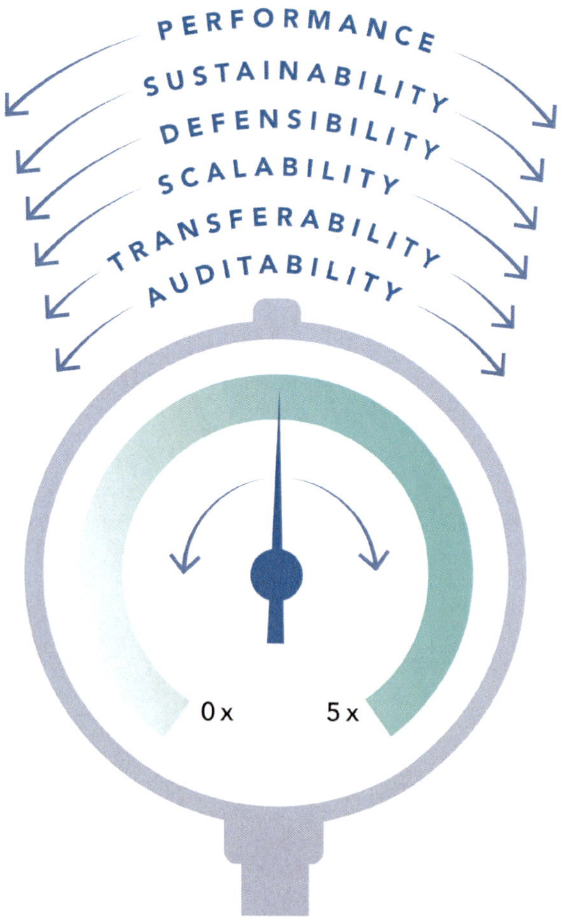

Find your Base Multiplier

Online businesses typically sell for an Earnings Multiplier of between 1x and 5x. So, if you multiply the Trailing 12 Months of Earnings by one and then by five, you can be reasonably confident that the current market value of your business falls between the resulting range. Of course this range is way too broad and doesn't tell you much at all. So let's look at some historical sales figures to hone in on the Base Multiplier.

Listing Price vs Sales Price

Don't make the mistake of confusing listing price (or asking price) with the actual sales price. Most publicly available data will give you the former rather than the latter. Anyone can list their business for a 5x Multiplier, but what was the highest bidder on the market actually willing to pay? And what were the deal terms? Generally speaking, businesses sell for between 10% and 20% below the listing price, but it can also be much, much less. Most brokers will admit to listing the business at 10%-20% above what they believe its true value is, but there are some that are guilty of inflating the listing price by a lot more. Then there's DIY marketplaces where the seller can list their business at any price they want. So if you're going to use publicly available data that only provides the listing price, it's safe to shave at least 15% off the price and even then take this data with a huge grain of salt.

To save you some homework, I have compiled and crunched *actual* sales data on more than 1,700 businesses sold between 2014 and 2021 by reputable marketplaces and brokers including Flippa, Empire Flippers and Dealflow. My hope is that one day everyone in the industry will agree to contribute their annual sales data to a peak body organization that can provide high quality, publicly available data to everyone. For now, the data I have compiled will have to do.

2.1 BUSINESS MODELS EXPLAINED

In the world of buying and selling online businesses, the term 'Business Model' specifically relates to the different ways in which a business is monetized. Each Business Model has a benchmark Valuation Multiplier, based on average historical sales figures. The five primary online Business Models are:

1. Saas
2. eCommerce
3. Content
4. Services
5. Transactional

Of course, many online Business Models incorporate multiple monetization methods, but there will usually be a primary Revenue stream, of which the Business Model is thus categorized. Consider Shopify for instance, which generates Revenue through subscriptions to their software (SaaS) as well as Merchant transaction fees (Transactional). Shopify is considered a SaaS business because its primary Revenue stream is through software subscriptions. The graph below displays the average Multiplier by Business Model for businesses sold between 2014 and 2021.

The reason Business Models have a big impact on value is because they are an indicator of other attributes, such as scarcity, scalability, predictability, or the skill/experience required to operate the business. As you might have guessed, the demand for each Business Model is not equal and is, therefore, a major reason why market average Multipliers vary significantly.

Some of these Business Models are subcategorized into more specific monetization methods. If you feel like you know everything there is to know about how online businesses are monetized and

2.1. BUSINESS MODELS EXPLAINED

	Multipliers							
Business Model	2014	2015	2016	2017	2018	2019	2020	2021
SaaS	2.83x	2.89x	3.17x	3.34x	3.55x	3.61x	3.79x	3.84x
eCommerce	2.56x	2.62x	2.67x	2.59x	2.70x	2.77x	2.94x	2.96x
Content	2.24x	2.31x	2.34x	2.39x	2.44	2.48x	2.56x	2.62x
Services	1.98x	2.21x	2.33x	2.29x	2.36x	2.34x	2.39x	2.47x
Transactional	2.61x	3.66x	3.59x	2.88x	2.92x	3.05x	3.23x	3.18x

Important reminder: Do not use this single data point to calculate the Base Multiplier or the Valuation of your business. You need to take into account all Base Multipliers Metrics in a single calculation.

why some yield higher Multipliers than others, feel free to jump ahead to 2.2 Business Size. The rest of you, onward!

2.1.1 SAAS

Software as a Service (SaaS) is where a service provider centrally hosts cloud-based software and licenses it to customers on a subscription basis. The provider holds full responsibility over the servers, database and data, thus enabling customers to save on infrastructure installation and maintenance costs. The monetization method for SaaS businesses is software subscription, providing access to services as long as the subscription remains active via recurring payments at selected intervals. With hundreds of SaaS sales reported across the industry in 2021, it can be concluded that SaaS businesses are typically the highest valued, mostly due to the predictable Revenue model and the ease of Scalability in comparison to other Business Models.

2.1.2 ECOMMERCE

An eCommerce company is a business primarily monetized through the sale of physical or digital products sold directly to customers via the internet. There are five main subtypes:

Physical Products eCommerce is where Revenue is generated from the sales of any tangible goods that require orders to be physically shipped to buyers and inventory to be replenished. Shoppers visit online stores to purchase literally any type of physical goods, such as clothing, groceries, tools, accessories, furniture, etc.. Once the commercial transaction has been completed online, the goods become available for collection or are delivered to the customer's door. For instance, Zappos.com delivers a wide range of footwear to countless shoppers via its online store.

Digital Products eCommerce is the sale of e-goods that can be sold repeatedly online without the need to replenish inventory. These goods can only be bought from a digital platform and can only be used on a digital device. Examples of e-goods include graphics, operating systems, softwares, video content, and music. Some businesses even offer a combination of digital and physical products. I have worked with dozens of clients who build industry-specific Wordpress theme templates and sell them through their online store.

Information Products eCommerce is where a business sells access to digital data and information meant for instructing, educating or guiding the consumer in order to meet a predefined purpose. The format of information products can be written, audio, video or a combination, and the aim is to address a challenge or a struggle the customer is looking to overcome. For example, Allen Carr's *Easy Way To Quit Smoking* is a non-fiction self-help book that has been converted into a digital eBook and a digital program with pre-recorded videos.

Subscription eCommerce is where a business provides ongoing products (both physical and digital) on a regular basis in exchange for regular payments from the customer. DollarShaveClub.com supplies thousands of customers with a shaving razor and other related products each month, and is an excellent example of a subscription e-commerce business. Historical sales data shows that subscription eCommerce businesses sell for a slightly higher Multiplier than other eCommerce subtypes. We can expect that this is due to the consistent and predictable nature of its income.

Dropship eCommerce involves a partnership between a dropshipper and a supplier, who takes care of the inventory, handling and delivery of the goods to the customers. In this case, all the dropshipper has to do is create an online platform for listing and selling the products, as well as handle the marketing side of things. When an order is received, they forward it to the supplier and keep the markup amount as commision. In short, dropshippers work as intermediaries between customers and suppliers. This Business Model has gained a lot of popularity lately, with most dropshippers setting up a quick store through websites like Shopify and using targeted Facebook Ads to drive Traffic and convert sales.

Fulfilment by Amazon (FBA) eCommerce involves selling products by using Amazon's website and vast network of distribution centers. All that's needed to set up a store is an agreement with a supplier for a high-selling product, and transportation to get the product from the factory to an Amazon-owned warehouse. The Amazon fulfilment centers handle the logistics, inventory, packing and shipment of the products for a fee, and you just have to ensure there is enough stock to meet the demand. Income is generated every time a shopper buys the product from your Amazon FBA listing. The already-established Traffic and loyal customer base of Amazon's website gives the business a launchpad, while the owner can focus on searching for profitable items and honing their marketing strategies.

2.1.3 CONTENT

Revenue is generated by monetizing website visitors through a number of avenues, including advertising, affiliate commissions, sponsorship and membership. There are three main subtypes:

Display Advertising relies on the paid, visual promotion of goods and services. A website owner might sell space to an advertiser for a determined period of time. This can be done either directly, or through an intermediary, like a targeted advertising network such as Google Adsense.

Affiliate Marketing, in its most basic form, is where a business creates promotional content about a product or service in exchange for a sales commission. Consider a technical expert in wireless headphones, who analyzes the leading products on his blog, which gets hundreds of thousands of hits a day. Everytime a reader clicks a link on the blog and is redirected to Sony's website where they purchase some headphones, Sony pays the blogger a commission. If the blogger didn't want to deal with a company like Sony directly, they could utilize an affiliate intermediary such as Amazon Associates, which operates much like Google Adsense.

Forums/Online Communities are monetized through user-generated content. Many forums are monetized through display advertising, while others generate Revenue through membership fees. In some cases, online community groups and forums make their money via sponsorship from large corporates. For example, a car manufacturing company might pay an auto mechanics' forum to create a focus group where the Users' valuable input might provide insight on specific changes they might want to consider for their product lines.

2.1.4 DIGITAL SERVICES

The term **Digital Services** refers to the electronic delivery of various types of services directly sold to customers via the internet. Unlike Digital Products, when you sell a service, you are trading your time for money and having to reproduce these efforts to more or less the same extent every time. Examples of Digital Services include content writing, copywriting, web design, digital marketing, and online tutoring. Typically, service-based businesses have the lowest value among the standard Business Models, because they are so often dependent on their operators, equating to a much higher risk profile than other models. If your business sells highly productized services with a subscription-based model, you can expect to sell for a higher Multiplier than a Pay-As-You-Go (PAYG) service that is fully customized. This is explored further in Chapter 6: Scalability.

2.1.5 TRANSACTIONAL

A Transactional business, otherwise known as a '*Marketplace Business*', is where Revenue is generated by facilitating user transactions on an online platform, in exchange for a fee or commission for each successful transaction. For a transactional business, the monetization method is the transaction itself and its success depends on its ability to create network effects. Two of the world's top online marketplaces are Amazon and eBay, who first introduced the model in the late 90s. PayPal, AliExpress, Etsy, Uber and AirBnB are examples of other thriving virtual marketplaces.

This Business Model is by far the rarest of the five, with only a few dozen acquisitions reported across the industry each year. This can largely be attributed to the frightfully high failure rate, with the vast majority of these businesses failing to achieve viability. The few that do manage to make a buck usually make a whole lot of them. Naturally, these rare gems tend to sell for a premium price tag.

2.2 BUSINESS SIZE

Looking at the graph below, it's clear that there is a linear relationship between Business Size and business value. That is to say: the bigger the business, the bigger the Multiplier. It is important to acknowledge that top-line Revenue is not always the best indicator of a business' size, but it's the best Metric we have to work with, so let's play on!

Why does a larger business generally yield a

2.2 BUSINESS SIZE

	Multipliers							
Annual Revenue	2014	2015	2016	2017	2018	2019	2020	2021
Less than $250K	2.33x	2.38x	2.37x	2.35x	2.48x	2.51x	2.56x	2.61x
$250K - $1M	2.42x	2.46x	2.47x	2.44x	2.52x	2.58x	2.64x	2.71x
$1M - $5M	2.63x	2.57x	2.72x	2.69x	2.78x	2.81x	2.85	2.99x
$5M - $25M	2.98x	3.02x	3.13x	3.23x	3.31x	3.36x	3.49x	3.52x
More than $25M	3.42x	3.50x	3.54x	3.47x	3.66x	3.54x	3.89x	3.91x

Important reminder: Do not use this single data point to calculate the Base Multiplier or the Valuation of your business. You need to take into account all Base Multipliers Metrics in a single calculation.

higher Valuation? Simple: *risk*. Larger businesses can weather the storm a lot easier than smaller businesses can. If there is a radical drop in sales, larger businesses have a lot more solutions available to them than smaller businesses that may not have many reserves or options to reduce operating costs until the storm passes. Another influencing factor is that Buyers stand to make significantly greater returns when they double the Earnings of an eight-figure business vs. a four-figure business. The graph below displays the average Multiplier by Business Size for businesses sold between 2014 and 2021.

2.3 BUSINESS AGE

The below graph shows that there is an ever-so-slight linear relationship between *business age* and *business value*. As you can see, the older the business, the bigger the Multiplier. A likely explanation for this is that because most businesses fail within three years, there is market disruption every other year and a recession every 10 years. In other words, a business that has passed the three-year hurdle, survived market disruptions and a recession, demonstrates a decent amount of *resilience*, making its risk profile smaller than if the business has only been operating for 13 months, say. One could go further and say a business that has been trading for several years likely has an established brand and customer base. With an established name in the market and a loyal customer base, older businesses are often granted a certain authority by consumers and search engines, making them more desirable to prospective buyers. The graph below displays the average Multiplier by business age for businesses sold between 2014 and 2021.

2.3 BUSINESS AGE

Multipliers

Business Age	2014	2015	2016	2017	2018	2019	2020	2021
1-2 Years	2.37x	2.36x	2.38x	2.42x	2.45x	2.51x	2.58x	2.57x
2-3 Years	2.51x	2.53x	2.61x	2.58x	2.63x	2.69x	2.74x	2.71x
3-5 Years	2.53x	2.61x	2.57x	2.59x	2.65x	2.67x	2.72x	2.74x
5-10 Years	2.59x	2.68x	2.64x	2.67x	2.73x	2.77x	2.84x	2.81x
10+ Years	2.70x	2.76x	2.73x	2.68x	2.75x	2.79x	2.88x	2.84x

Important reminder: Do not use this single data point to calculate the Base Multiplier or the Valuation of your business. You need to take into account all Base Multipliers Metrics in a single calculation.

2.4 OWNER TIME COMMITMENT

The below graph shows that there are the markings of a linear relationship between Owner Time Commitment and business value. As you can see, the lower the owner's weekly time commitment, the bigger the Multiplier. That's because *time is an Asset* and thus the more hours it takes the acquirer to run the business, the lower his hourly rate becomes. The graph on the following page displays the average Multiplier by Owner Time Commitment for businesses sold between 2014 and 2021.

If you're wondering why a business that takes less than 5 hours a week only sells for a slightly higher Multiplier than one that takes 30+ hours a week to run - it is probably because buyers are aware that owner time commitment is often misrepresented and may not necessarily take them less than 5 hours a week to run the business. However, if your business is truly a highly passive business, you can expect to sell for a significantly higher Multiplier (all other things equal).

2.4 OWNER TIME COMMITMENT

Multipliers

	2014	2015	2016	2017	2018	2019	2020	2021
< 5 Hours	2.62x	2.67x	2.66x	2.69x	2.76x	2.84x	2.87x	2.85x
5-10 Hours	2.55x	2.58x	2.62x	2.65x	2.68x	2.79x	2.76x	2.74x
10-20 Hours	2.57x	2.59x	2.58x	2.64x	2.67x	2.72x	2.77x	2.76x
20-30 Hours	2.44x	2.48x	2.52x	2.57x	2.64x	2.59x	2.73x	2.72x
30+ Hours	2.46x	2.54x	2.53x	2.55x	2.58x	2.61x	2.65x	2.66x

Important reminder: Do not use this single data point to calculate the Base Multiplier or the Valuation of your business. You need to take into account all Base Multipliers Metrics in a single calculation.

ACTIVITY 2

Figure out your Base Multiplier

Considering all of the above, you should now be able to get a decent idea of what your Base Multiplier is. The diagram below demonstrates this perfectly by showing that a large, well-established SaaS business requiring minimal owner involvement is likely to sell for a much higher

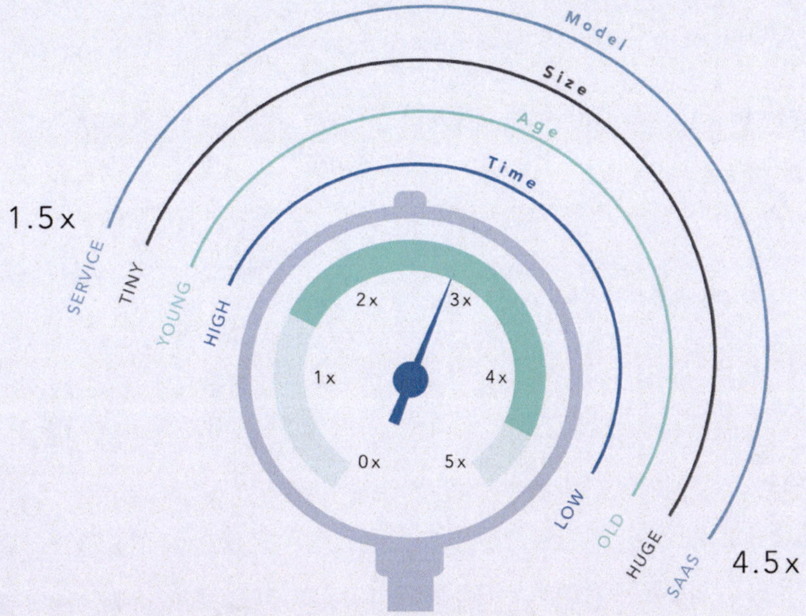

Multiplier than a small, young and onerous Services business.

Because the limited data set we are working with does not separate *Business Size, Business Age* and *Time Commitment* data by each Business Model, we cannot simply calculate Business Model x Business Size x Business Age x Time Commitment and then divide by four. Hopefully the key players in our industry come together to create a comprehensive historical sales report. Until that time, we have to work with whatever data and common sense we have.

1. Take the 2021 Multiplier for your business model. Depending on the specific monetization type (e.g. FBA, Subscription eCommerce, etc.) you may wish to adjust this number slightly by "0.1" in either direction.

2. Reference the diagram above, as well as the *Size, Age* and *Time* data tables to get a sense for whether your Multiplier is likely to increase or decrease.

    a. *Business Size* won't create any Downward Pressure on your Multiplier, but if your business generates $5M+ in revenue, you could safely add a small bonus of +0.1 to +0.3x to your Multiplier.

    b. *Business Age* can create Upward and Downward Pressure on your Multiplier. If your business is less than 12 months old, the uncertainty around future performance will create significant Downward Pressure on your Multiplier and may be difficult to sell at all. Conversely, if your business is 5+ years old, you can safely add a small bonus of +0.1x or +0.3x to your Multiplier.

    c. *Time Commitment* has a very minimal impact on your Multiplier, if it truly takes you less than 10 hours a week to run your business you can add +0.1 or +0.2 to your Multiplier, because many buyers are happy to pay a premium for less laborious investment.

3. Write down your estimated Base Multiplier

____

Now that you have established your ballpark Base Multiplier, we can hone in further on the other six Value Pressures and explore how they impact your business' Valuation.

KEY TAKEAWAYS

BASE MULTIPLIER

- When valuing a business using the Earnings Multiplier method, you need a starting point from which to base your Valuation. This is called the Base Multiplier.

- The Base Multiplier is determined by benchmarking historical sales and Valuation data on four key factors:
    - **Business Model**
    - **Business Size**
    - **Business Age**
    - **Owner Time Commitment**

- Do not, under any circumstance, use a single component (such as Business Size) to calculate the Base Multiplier or the Valuation of your business. You need to take into account all Base Multipliers Metrics in a single calculation:
    - **(Business Model + Business Size + Business Age + Owner Commitment) ÷ 4**

- The reason why Business Models have a big impact on value is because they are an indicator of other attributes, such as scarcity, Scalability, predictability, or the skill/experience required to operate them.
    - SaaS businesses yield high Multiples because they are scalable and predictable.
    - Transactional businesses sell for high Multiples because they are scarce and defensible.
    - Content and eCommerce businesses are extremely popular in the market and sell for lower multiples than SaaS or Transactional because they aren't generally as scarce, scalable, or predictable.
    - Services businesses often yield the lowest Multiplier because they are typically dependent on their owners and relatively difficult to scale.
    - Long-established businesses often sell for higher Multiples than their younger counterparts because they have proven their resilience through virtue of surviving market volatility.

- Although **Business Size** does not influence the Multiplier as much as the Business Model does, larger businesses tend to sell for higher Multiples because they are generally considered to be more resilient during adverse market conditions. Buyers also stand to make significantly greater returns when they double the Earnings of an eight-figure business vs. a four-figure business

- **Business Age** has a greater impact on the Multiplier than Business Size, but still less so than the Business Model. Buyers are aware that nine out of 10 businesses fail in the first three years and there is market disruption or a recession every 10 years. Therefore, the longer your business has been around, the less risky the acquisition of your business seems to be, placing upward pressure on the Multiplier.

- The lesser the **Owner's Time Commitment**, the less time a Buyer has to spend getting a good return on their investment, creating upward pressure on the Multiplier.

GAUGING PERFORMANCE

3

3. GAUGING PERFORMANCE

In this Chapter, we will learn about the most impactful Pressure Gauge - *performance*. When prospective buyers are skimming through a sales prospectus, they will usually skip straight to the performance section. Why? Because performance determines the future Cash Flow of a business. In other words, it helps the buyer determine the time, effort, and resources required to recuperate their initial investment, as well as maintaining or growing the business' value in the future.

Performance = Future Cash Flow
= Return on Investment (ROI)

Performance Pressures create equally as much Downward Pressure as Upward Pressure on the Multiplier

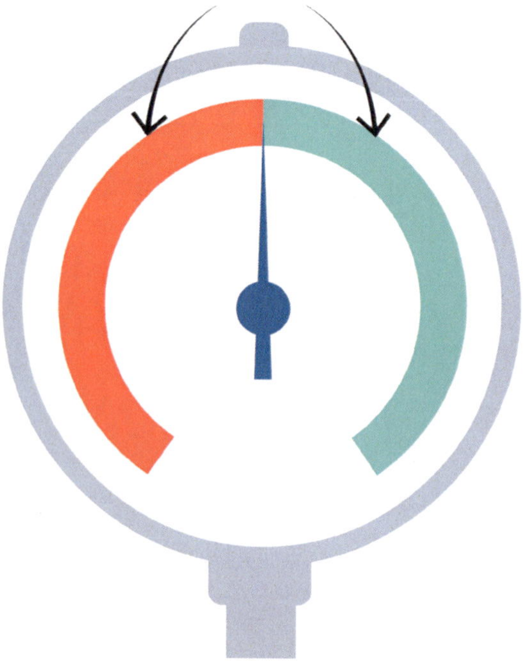

As you can see in the diagram above, your performance can create significant pressure in both directions, depending on how your business scores against the mean.

For example, if the business in question is trending downwards, then the rate of return is likely to be slower, making the business less desirable than a business trending upwards and projecting quicker rates of return. To accurately identify performance Trends, you must first understand how the three modes of performance intersect and influence one another. The three modes of performance are:

- Current Performance
- Past Performance
- Future Performance

The other reason performance has the greatest influence on value compared to other drivers is because it can be measured by analyzing raw data Metrics, as opposed to more subjective and speculative factors that we will explore later on.

While performance Metrics will vary depending on the Business Model, buyers will look to analyze Trends in the following key areas:

- Financial Performance (Revenue Trend, Gross Profit %, Earnings Trend, etc.)
- Web Traffic Performance (Bounce Rate Trend, Sessions Trend, Session Duration Trend, etc.)
- Customer Performance (Repeat Customer Rate %, Churn Rate, Customer Lifetime Value, etc.)
- Marketing Performance (Email Open Rate, Advertising ROI, Link Profile, etc.)

Before we delve into specific performance Metrics, let's quickly touch on the relationship between current, past and future performance.

3.1 CURRENT PERFORMANCE

Buyers will generally pay closest attention to how the business is currently performing because it paints the most accurate picture of its current health and condition. Although yesterday's sales technically fall under the category of 'past performance', we typically consider the Trailing Twelve Months (TTM) to be the standard measurement of current performance. As stated above in section 1.4.2 TTM refers to the past Twelve consecutive *completed* months. For instance, if the current date was July 9th 2022, TTM would be July 1st 2021 to June 30th 2022. You don't typically report the current month the business is in because there isn't a full month's worth of data.

Trailing Six Months (T6M) and Trailing Three Months (T3M) are timeframes that are used to measure *current performance* when a younger business has less than 12 months of Profit history or when a business is experiencing rapid growth or decline. When applying T6M or T3M methods, the average monthly Earnings over that time period must be extrapolated (*annualized*) to represent a 12-month period.

While current performance has a significant impact on Valuation, it doesn't always give us the full picture of how your business is really performing.

TRAILING THREE MONTHS CALCULATION

Month	Sep 21	Oct 21	Nov 21
Earnings	$5,000	$7,000	$6,000

Calculating:

1. Sum total of T3M: $5,000 + $7,000 + $6,000 = $18,000
2. Divide total by number of months to get T3M average: $18,000 ÷ 3 = $6,000
3. Annualize by multiplying T3M average by 12: $6,000 x 12 = $72,000

3.2 PAST PERFORMANCE

Comparing historical performance with current performance lets us determine how a business is *trending*. Let's consider two software companies that earned the same amount of money during the same 12-month period.

CURRENT PERFORMANCE

	Company A	vs	Company B
Model	SaaS		SaaS
Founded	2015		2015
Earnings	$500,000		$500,000

If we only consider current performance, we would obviously conclude that the two companies are worth the same amount. *Now let's now look at their past performance.*

PAST PERFORMANCE

	Company A	vs	Company B
2019	$2,000,000		$125,000
2020	$1,000,000		$250,000
2021	$500,000		$500,000

HISTORICAL PERFORMANCE

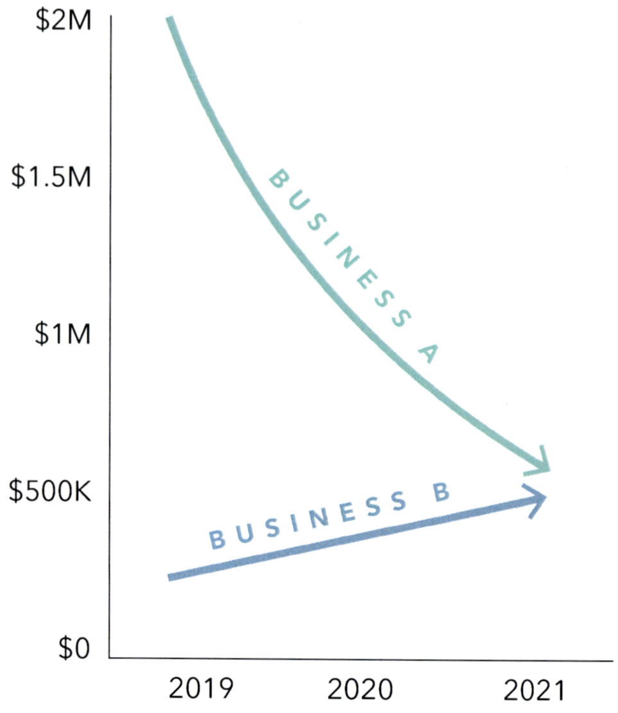

Which business would you rather buy? You would pick Business B, right? Me too. Business A makes me *very* nervous, whereas Business B looks like it's got a bright future ahead.

How much would you pay for Business A vs. Business B? If it were me, I'd be willing to pay a lot more for Business B. If the growth rates of both companies continue on their current trajectory and I paid a 1x Multiplier for Business A, and 4x Multiplier for Business B, I would still make a faster and much bigger return on Business B three years from now.

By 2022, Business B will start earning more than Business A.

HOW MUCH WOULD YOU PAY FOR BUSINESS A VS. BUSINESS B?

	Business A Approx. Growth Rate: -30% Purchase Price: $500,000 Multiplier: 1x		vs	Business B Approx. Growth Rate: 100% Purchase Price: $2,000,000 Multiplier: 4x	
	Earnings	**ROI**		**Earnings**	**ROI**
Time of Purchase	$500,000	-$500,000		$500,000	-$2,000,000
Year 1	$250,000	-$250,000		$1,000,000	-$1,000,000
Year 2	$125,000	-$125,000		$2,000,000	$1,000,000
Year 3	$62,500	-$62,500		$4,000,000	$5,000,000

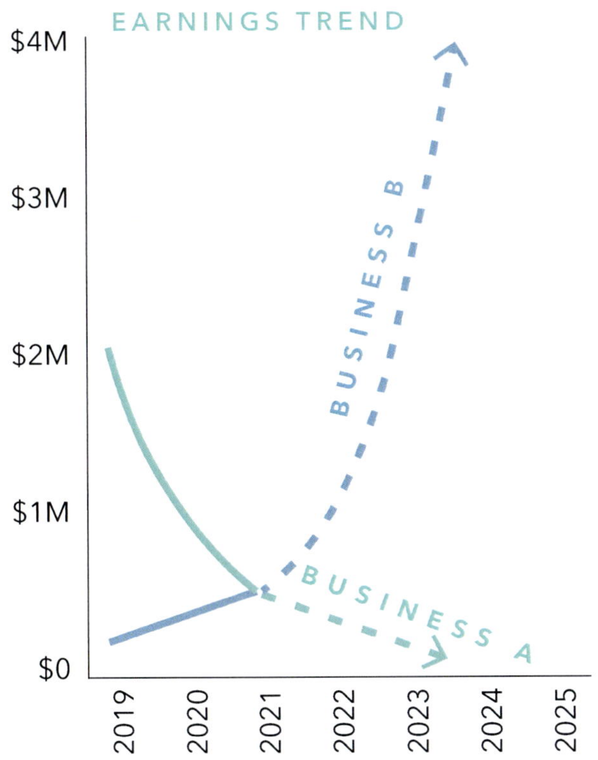

Business B will break even before Business A.

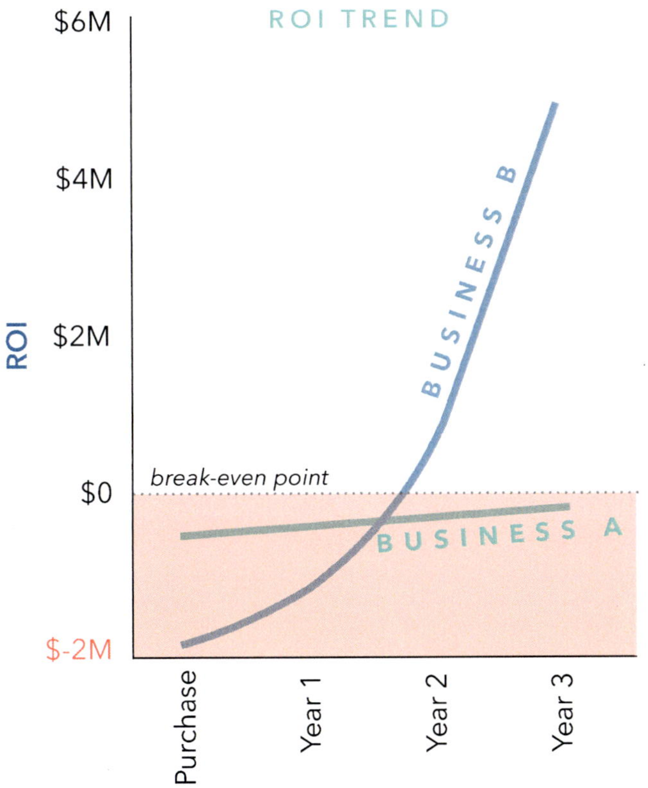

This example would indicate that Business B is in fact far more than 4x as valuable as Business A. But how do you know that Business B will continue doubling its Earnings year after year? You don't. In fact, it could start to plateau or decline tomorrow. So how *does* one accurately measure future performance?

3.3 FUTURE PERFORMANCE

Put simply, future performance is what everyone is trying to figure out. It's the key ingredient that determines the value of your online business. The punchline is, of course, that future performance can only be speculative because the future is the future - *it hasn't happened yet*. However, as exemplified above, we know that current and past performance can help us to identify positive (Business B) and negative (Business A) growth Trends. We also know that positive and negative growth Trends impact value in opposing ways and largely determine the projected future performance, Cash Flow and therefore, value of a business.

However, growth Trends do not tell us *everything* we need to know to accurately estimate future performance. There are many other factors, both internal and external, that influence projections by valuers and Buyers alike. After looking at some of the most influential performance Metrics in this Chapter, the rest of this book will teach you about the other Value Pressures and how they impact future performance and online business value.

Now that you know how past, current and future performance are interconnected, let's look at some of the financial, Traffic, customer and marketing Metrics that are most commonly used to evaluate the performance of online businesses.

3.4 FINANCIAL PERFORMANCE METRICS

Financial performance acts as an umbrella and a *catch-all* for all the performance Metrics because every other Metric influences how a business performs financially in one way or another. That is to say that a business with a high repeat customer rate or a high volume of engaged social media followers will directly or indirectly influence sales revenue, margins, operating costs, and profitability - hence why buyers often analyze financial performance Metrics before delving deeper into other Metrics. Let's look at some of the most prominent financial Metrics in the table on the following page.

Revenue Trend

The increase (or decrease) in sales income from one period to the next is a very simple way of determining how a business is trending.

Up = good
Down = bad
Plateau = acceptable to some, not to others.

ARR / MRR Trend

For subscription businesses with recurring revenue models, the Trends in Annual Recurring Revenue (ARR) and Monthly Recurring Revenue (MRR) are tell-tale Metrics that provide an instant snapshot of how a business is performing.

ARR = revenue from annual or multi-year* subscribers ($100,000) + upgrades / add-ons ($10,000) - losses from downgrades or lost customers ($5,000) over the Trailing Twelve Months (TTM) period.

$100,000 + $10,000 - $5,000 = $105,000 ARR

** If customers buy multi-year contracts with customers then divide the contract value by the number of years.*

MRR = number of active monthly subscribers (100) x average monthly subscription billing amount ($10).

100 x $10 = $1,000 MRR

ARR / MRR** Trend = [Year 2 Revenue ($105,000) - Year 1 Revenue ($95,000)] ÷ Year 1 Revenue ($95,000) x 100

($105,000 - $95,000) ÷ $95,000 x 100 = 16.7%

*** For MRR, you can choose to use this same formula and apply it to the Trailing 3,6, or 12 months.*

Gross Profit %

The amount of money left over from sales after deducting the direct cost of goods and services sold (CoGS). Higher margins generally mean better Cash Flow and greater flexibility with operational spend. Conversely, lower margins leave little meat on the bone to invest in growth. The formula is expressed as follows:

Revenue - CoGS ÷ Revenue - Gross Profit %

Earnings Trend

The increase (or decrease) in money the owner(s) make from one period to the next is the financial Metric Investors are most concerned with because it is a strong indicator of what future performance might look like. If operating costs are increasing at a faster rate than revenue, then Profits will drop and projections of future Earnings won't look as promising.

Earnings (SDE) = Revenue - Cost of Goods Sold - Expenses + Owner Compensation + Unnecessary Costs

Earnings Trend = [Year 2 SDE ($80,000) - Year 1 Earnings ($60,000)] ÷ Year 1 Earnings ($60,000) x 100

($80,000 - $60,000) ÷ $60,000 x 100 = 33.3%

3.5 WEB TRAFFIC PERFORMANCE METRICS

Web Traffic provides you (as well as prospective buyers) with vital information on how people arrive on your site and how they engage with its content. There are dozens of Web Traffic Metrics you can track. But some are more important than others. The table below lists four Metrics that almost every Buyer or valuer will analyze when determining the value of your business.

Google Analytics (GA) is widely considered to be the most comprehensive web Traffic analytics platform. If you don't have Google Analytics (properly!) installed on your website, it will be very difficult to sell your business, because most Buyers and valuers will require at least 12 months of Google Analytics data. So if you haven't got Google Analytics installed, add it to the list of things to do as soon as you put this book down.

Monthly Users Trend

Comparing the volume of Users that engage with your website from month to month can be a useful way to gauge the health of an online business. If fewer people are visiting your website each month, there are fewer opportunities to sell your product or service (or advertising space). Google Analytics applies a unique identifier code to each User via browser cookies. This helps distinguish new Users from returning ones.

1. Go to analytics.google.com > Audience > Active Users
2. Adjust the date range over a 3,6,or 12 month period and study the trend line.

Sessions Trend

A Session is a period of time during which a User engages with your website. By analyzing Users and Sessions together, you can get a sense for how many times the average User visits your website in a given month. For instance, if there are 500 Users and 1,000 Sessions, then the average User visits your site twice every month. The calculation thus looks like this:

1,000 Sessions ÷ 500 Users = 2 Sessions Per User

More Sessions means more activity, which is generally positive, although it won't always necessarily result in more sales.

1. Go to analytics.google.com > Audience > Overview
2. Adjust the date range over a 3,6,or 12 month period and study the trend line.

Bounce Rate Trend

Bounce Rate represents the percentage of Users who enter your website and "bounce" off without interacting (clicking, visiting another page, etc.). Bounce rate is calculated by dividing the total number of *Single Page Sessions* by the total number of *Sessions* on your website. For example, if 10 Users visit your website and three of them "bounce" without clicking to another page, then your Bounce Rate will be 30%. We're generally cautious of Bounce Rates higher than 75%, because this could indicate that the majority of visitors to your website are not interested in what they find. Generally speaking, the lower the Bounce Rate, the better.

1. Go to analytics.google.com > Audience > Active Users
2. Adjust the date range over a 3,6,or 12 month period and study the trend line.

Avg. Session Duration Trend	
	The average duration of a Session is another important Metric because it shows how long people tend to stay on your website. This is possibly one of the truest indicators of User engagement on a website. A Session count starts the moment a User enters your website, and ends when the User either leaves the site, or after a specified amount of time passes where no interactions take place. If a sports blog has an average session duration time of 30 seconds, then it would indicate that readers aren't really engaging with the content. However, a health blog with an average session duration time of five minutes suggests that readers enjoy the content. Obviously, it is much easier to monetize an engaged audience, making the health blog a much more attractive acquisition. 1. Go to analytics.google.com > Audience > Active Users 2. adjust the date range over a 3,6,or 12 month period and study the trend line.

The above table is by no means an exhaustive list of website Traffic Metrics, but should give you an idea of how you (or potential Buyers) can assess the quality and effectiveness of your web design, content, functionality and marketing initiatives by looking at Google Analytics reports over different date ranges.

3.6 CUSTOMER PERFORMANCE METRICS

While Traffic performance Metrics tell us about how Users are interacting with your website, Customer Performance Metrics tell us about how customers are transacting with your business. To solidify this distinction, think of Traffic as all the people that enter a clothing store and browse around. Now think of customers as the people who purchase a T-shirt or sweater. Naturally, there is a lot of overlap and interconnectivity between these two Metrics, as they both relate to the behavior of both customers and potential customers. By comparing Traffic data and transactional customer data, you can establish the Conversion Rate of certain Traffic sources and marketing activities.

Repeat Customer Rate %

The Repeat Customer Rate measures the number of customers that return to purchase an additional product or service provided by the site after their initial transaction is completed. This percentage is obtained by dividing the number of returning customers by the total number of customers.

Repeat Customer Rate = (Repeat Customers ÷ Total Customers) x 100

If 50 out of 100 customers purchased from you two or more times, your repeat customer rate would be 50%.

(50 ÷ 100) x 100 = 50%.

Generally speaking, a high repeat customer rate is a strong indicator that your product or service is high quality, which buyers will no doubt consider favorably when valuing your business.

Purchase Frequency

Purchase Frequency measures the average number of times a customer makes a purchase within a specific period of time. It is calculated by dividing the total number of orders by the total number of unique customers in the same time period, as follows:

Purchase Frequency = Number of Orders ÷ Number of Unique Customers

If your business had 500 orders in the past 12 months and 100 unique customers, then your average purchase frequency is five (500 ÷ 100 = 5).

Churn Rate %

Churn Rate is a Metric used for subscription-based businesses and is the percentage of customers that unsubscribe from your service over a specific time period. There are several ways to calculate churn, but the simplest one is as follows:

Churn Rate = Number of Churned Customers ÷ Total Number of Customers

In this calculation, the *number of churned customers* represents the amount of subscribers out of your *total number of customers* within a given time period who stopped doing business with you by discontinuing or not renewing their subscriptions.

For example, if 50 Users unsubscribed from your platform out of a total of 1,000, your Churn Rate would be 0.05, or 5% (50 ÷ 1,000 = 0.05).

Average Order Value (AOV)

Average Order Value is a Metric commonly used in eCommerce businesses, as it measures the average value of a customer's purchase orders over a specific period of time. It is calculated by dividing Revenue by the number of total orders. It is important in eCommerce, because it will provide marketing teams insights when it comes to advertising spend, pricing of products and promotions. The formula to find the AOV is:

AOV = Revenue ÷ # of Orders

For example, if you had a revenue of $20,000 and a total order count of 2,000, your Average Order Value would be $10. Some buyers (but not all) prefer businesses with a large AOV because every new customer acquired represents a significant increase in revenue.

Average Revenue Per User (ARPU)

ARPU is one of the most important Metrics in online businesses, as it measures the monetary Profit that a business can expect to generate from a single customer over a given time period. ARPU is calculated as follows:

ARPU = Total Revenue ÷ Total Users During a Specific Period of Time

For example, if you have a total monthly Revenue of $500,000 and 10,000 Users, your monthly ARPU would be $50 ($500,000 ÷ 10,000 = $50).

Customer Acquisition Cost (CAC)

Customer Acquisition Cost is the dollar amount that a company spends to gain a paying customer. This allows you to determine whether your sales and marketing efforts are producing a positive or negative return. The formula to calculate the CAC is as follows:

CAC = (Total Cost of Sales And Marketing) ÷ (# of Customers Acquired)

For example, if you spent $50,000 in marketing wages and advertising spend to acquire 5,000 new customers, then your CAC would be $10 (50,000 ÷ 5,000 = 10). As long as your Customer Lifetime Value (CLV) is more than $10, then you are making a positive return on your marketing efforts. The lower your CAC and the higher your CLV, the more lucrative your business will appear to buyers and potential Investors.

Lifetime Value (LTV)

The Lifetime Value Metric is the total Revenue a business can reasonably expect to earn from a single customer over the lifetime of their relationship.

LTV = Average Order Value (AOV) x Average Number of Transactions Over Lifetime

The calculation will vary depending on the type of business you own. For instance, if you own an eCommerce business, then you will multiply your Average Order Value (AOV) by your Average Purchase Frequency:

LTV = AOV x Purchase Frequency x Retention Time Period

If AOV is $50, your purchase frequency is 2 and the average Retention Time Period is 2, then your LTV is $200 ($50 x 2 x 2 = $200).

However, if you own a SaaS business, you will divide your Average Revenue Per User (ARPU) by your Churn Rate %:

LTV = ARPU ÷ Churn Rate %

If ARPU is $100 and your Churn Rate is 5%, then your LTV is $2,000 ($100 ÷ 5% = $2,000).

Customer Lifetime Value (CLV)

Customer Lifetime Value (CLV) is different to Lifetime Value (LTV) because LTV measures the *gross* value of a customer, whereas CLV measures the *net* value of a customer. The simplest way to calculate CLV is by subtracting the average Customer Acquisition Cost (CAC) from the average Lifetime Value (LTV).

CLV = LTV - CAC

If your LTV is $1,000 and your CAC is $100, then your CLV is $900 ($1,000 - $100 = $900).

LTV:CAC Ratio

The CAC:LTV Ratio is pretty self explanatory. You simply divide CLV by CAC to establish the ratio between them:

LTV:CAC Ratio = LTV / CAC

So, if your Customer Lifetime Value is $4,000 and your Customer Acquisition Cost is $1,000, then your LTV:CAC ratio would be 4:1 [$4,000/$1,000)/1000]. A ratio of 1:1 would mean that you're spending the same amount of money acquiring a customer as they will spend with your business in their lifetime. This, of course, would be effectively pointless, the business won't profit a single penny from that customer. Generally speaking, a healthy LTV:CAC ratio is considered to 3:1 and above. because

Refund Rate %

As its name indicates, the Refund Rate is the percentage of transactions that are returned to the client. Depending on the service provided, some businesses will have higher Refund Rates than others, but the rule of thumb is that the lower the rate, the better the product quality or service. That being said, a well-managed refund policy can be an effective marketing tool. The online shoe retailer Zappos offers a 365-day, free two-way shipping and return policy. The company states that while their most loyal customers often return pairs of shoes, they are also the ones that spend the most on the website, and are the most profitable customers.

Refund Rate % = Total Refunds ÷ Total Orders

If you suspect you might have a refund problem, try to uncover the underlying issue. *Does the product or service you provide match your description? Are products arriving late? Do you need to review your refund policy?*

Customer Review Rating

A Customer Review can hold the same importance to an online business as a personal recommendation. Good reviews show the business in a positive light, while a significant number of negative reviews will hinder a business's ability to build a loyal customer base.

For obvious reasons, Buyers prefer businesses with positive reviews rather than negative ones. If your business is struggling with negative reviews and your overall Customer Review rating is below 4/5, see 4.1 for advice on how to improve the public profile of your business.

Net Promoter Score (NPS)

An essential customer Metric used by the vast majority of Fortune 500 companies for measuring customer loyalty is the Net Promoter Score (NPS). This Metric asks one simple question: "From one to 10, how likely are you to recommend our company/product/services to a friend or colleague?"

Responses between 0-6 are considered detractors, while 7-8 are passives, and 9-10 are designated as promoters of that business. A business' NPS can be between -100 and +100.

An NPS of 0 is deemed to be decent by most standards, and a score of +50 is considered outstanding. However, it should be noted that there are some serious limitations to this Metric, and in order to get a more accurate feel for your customers' level of loyalty, you need to drill down deeper and get a bit more specific.

If you don't currently track your NPS, there are many NPS tools and plugins that are quick, easy and affordable to integrate.

3.7 MARKETING PERFORMANCE METRICS

Marketing performance Metrics allow us to track and measure the effectiveness of particular marketing initiatives, activities and campaigns. Although Financial, Traffic and Customer Metrics all provide invaluable insight into how a business' marketing operations are performing, there are specific Metrics that will help buyers determine whether a particular marketing channel has been exhausted or under-utilized. Particular channels that are under-performing or have been under-utilized may represent an opportunity for prospective buyers to improve performance. Conversely, marketing channels that have been exhausted may indicate to Buyers that there is little that can be done to improve performance further. Amongst other channels, we will take a deep dive into the key marketing Metrics of four primary channels: Email, Advertising, Social and Content.

3.7.1 EMAIL MARKETING METRICS

Email marketing relates to emails and newsletters sent to people who have subscribed to your business' email list. Below are a handful of Metrics that are commonly used to assess the performance of email marketing campaigns:

Open Rate %

The Open Rate Metric is a key performance indicator in email marketing, as it tracks the percentage of email recipients who actually open a given email. Businesses use the Open Rate to assess how interested or uninterested their subscribers are in what the company has to say.

The most accurate formula for calculating your Open Rate is:

(Total Emails Opened ÷ [Total Emails Sent - Bounced Emails]) x 100

For example, if you've sent out 100 emails and 15 of them bounced, the number of delivered emails becomes 85. If, out of those emails, 40 were opened, then your Open Rate is 40 ÷ 85 = 0.47 x 100 = 47%

The average Open Rate will vary depending on what market your business operates in. According to MailChimp however, the average Open Rate across all industries is 21.3%.

Clickthrough Rate (CTR) %

This Metric is used to determine the success of an email campaign, by measuring the percentage of email recipients who clicked on the links included in a given email. The CTR provides direct insight into the amount of subscribers who actively engage with the company's content and display interest in finding out more about the brand's profile and offers.

Before calculating your CTR, it is important to decide how you define a 'click' – do you measure individual clicks or clicks by an individual person?

As long as you choose one way for consistency purposes, you can then apply your numbers to the following formula:

CTR = Number of Clicks ÷ Total Emails Opened x 100

For example, if your total clicks were 25, and 500 emails were opened, then your CTR is 5% (25 ÷ 500 = 0.05 x 100)

Although this varies considerably depending on the marketing you operate in, if your CTR is above 3%, you are doing better than average, and if it's below 1% it's time to re-evaluate your engagement strategy or simply scrub your email list.

Unsubscribe Rate %

The Unsubscribe Rate is the percentage of Users who have opted-out from your mailing list, and it is a good Metric to track after every email campaign.

The calculation formula is:

Unsubscribe Rate = (Unsubscribes ÷ Successful Email Deliveries) x 100

For example, if 5,000 emails were successfully delivered as part of your campaign and 15 Users unsubscribed, then your Unsubscribe Rate would be 0.3% (15 ÷ 5,000 = 0.003 x 100).

On one hand, unsubscribes are almost like a self-cleaning of your mailing list from uninterested prospects. However, a high Unsubscribe Rate can damage your sender reputation and result in negative consequences from email service providers like Outlook, Gmail, and Yahoo.

Unsubscribe Rates below 0.5% are considered normal, while rates of 0.2% and below are excellent. If your Unsubscribe Rate is more than 0.5%, perhaps it's time you revised your email marketing strategy.

It is also important to remember that Unsubscribe Rates for newly generated mailing lists are naturally higher than for ones that have reached a certain level of maturity, as at this point, a company is still in the process of building relationships with its leads.

List Growth Rate %

The List Growth Rate Metric describes the rate at which a business' email list is growing. Companies use this Metric to keep track of their list's growth and losses. A high List Growth Rate indicates that a business' email marketing strategies are successful in expanding its audience, extending its reach, and maintaining a healthy list size. That being said, it is also important to acknowledge that an email subscriber is very different to a paying customer.

This is the formula for calculating your List Growth Rate:

(Number Of New Subscribers - Number of Unsubscribes) ÷ Total Number of Email Addresses on Your List x 100

For example if you had 40 new subscribers, five unsubscribes, and a total of 350 emails on your list, then your List Growth Rate would be 10% ((40-5) ÷ 350 = 0.1 x 100).

Conversion Rate %

The Conversion Rate Metric refers to the percentage of email recipients who clicked on the link contained in an email, and then proceeded to complete a specific action - usually a purchase or filling out a form. Conversion Rates are an important measure of success regarding a company newsletters' effectiveness in actually generating prospects and leads.

(Number of Converted Sales from Recipients ÷ Number of Emails) x 100

To calculate your Conversion Rate, you need to divide the number of conversions by the number of delivered emails and multiply it by 100. Let's say you sent out 2,000 promotional emails and 137 recipients completed a purchase - then your Conversion Rate would be 6.85% (137÷ 2,000 = 0.0685 x 100).

Buyers will analyze historical performance to determine how your Conversion Rate is trending, as well as your Customer Channels (4.3) to establish how easily your Conversion Rate can be improved.

Email ROI %

This Metric measures the overall ROI for a business' email campaigns. Put simply, it's the campaign's total Revenue divided by total spend. Depending on the Business Model, there are several ways to calculate the ROI of an email campaign. The basic formula is as follows:

Email ROI ($) = Email Campaign Revenue - Campaign Costs

Email ROI % = (Email Campaign Revenue - Campaign Costs) ÷ Amount Spent x 100

Let's say that over the Trailing Twelve Months your email campaigns have generated $40,000. During that same time period, you spent $1,200 on your email service provider subscription and $7,800 on paying your email marketer for 5 hours a week at $30/hour, totalling $9,000 in email campaign costs.

Your ROI would be $31,000 (($40,000 - $9,000 = $31,000) and your ROI % would be 344.4% [($40,000 - $9,000) ÷ $9,000 x 100]).

3.7.2 PAID ADVERTISING METRICS

Paid advertising is where businesses pay search engines (Google, Bing), social media platforms (Facebook, Instagram, Youtube) and other websites to promote their offering. Some businesses use ad networks, while others strike up an ad deal directly with the website owner. Here are some of the most important Metrics to track and measure:

PAID ADVERTISING METRICS

Advertising ROI

The most basic way to calculate the Advertising ROI of a marketing campaign is by subtracting the marketing costs from the sales growth of the business or product, and dividing that number by the marketing cost.

Advertising ROI = (Sales Growth - Marketing Cost) ÷ Marketing Cost

In an optimistic scenario, let's say, that your sales grew by $3,000 and the cost of the marketing campaign was $300, then the equation would be:

ROI = [($3,000-$300) / $300] = 900%

However, to clearly determine the campaign's impact – and for the Advertising ROI to have any realistic meaning – it is important to compare sales from the business or product prior to launching the ad campaign. For example, you can calculate the existing sales Trend with a 12-month campaign lead up.

If over that 12-month period, your sales show an average organic growth rate of 5% per month, then your campaign's Advertising ROI calculation should exclude that 5% from the sales growth. Taking out organic growth will bring a more modest (but more realistic) ROI. The formula is as follows:

ROI = (Sales Growth - Average Organic Sales Growth - Marketing Cost) ÷ Marketing Cost

Cost Per Acquisition (CPA)

Cost Per Acquisition (CPA) is a Metric that measures the total cost advertisers pay to acquire one paying customer. The thing that distinguishes it from CAC is its detailed campaign-level application. Equipped with the Average Order Value (AOV) and Customer Lifetime Value (CLV) we studied in 3.6, Buyers will establish whether your CPA is healthy or unsustainable. The formula for calculating CPA is:

CPA = Total Campaign Cost ÷ Conversions

For instance, if you spent $1,000 in your latest campaign and acquired 35 new customers during that period, then your CPA is $28.57 ($1,000 / 35).

Conversion Rate (CVR)

Conversion Rate (CVR) is the best way to measure the financial performance of your advertising campaigns, and the main reason you invested in them in the first place. Put simply, CVR is the percentage of Users who were converted by your ad through responding to and completing your call-to-action – be it a purchase, subscription, form submission, etc.

Basically, your CVR measures your campaign's success in progressing a potential customer along the funnel towards becoming a paying customer, which is why campaign managers always keep a close eye on Conversions. Most online advertising and analytics platforms (Google Ads, Google Analytics, Facebook Ads etc.) can display your CVR in their interface if you set up your tracking correctly. However, if you want to calculate your CVR manually, the formula is:

$$\text{CVR} = (\text{Conversions} \div \text{Total Visitors}) \times 100$$

For example, if, during a given time frame, your Conversions were 1,067, and your total visitors were 8,748, then your CVR for that period was 12.19% (1067 / 8748 = 0.1219 x 100).

Cost Per Thousand Impressions (CPM) Trend

Cost Per Thousand Impressions (CPM) is the most commonly used method in digital marketing when it comes to pricing web ads. CPM denotes the set fee an advertiser pays for every 1,000 ad Impressions – also known as 'ad views' – on a web page. For example, if an online publisher charges $5.00 CPM, that means an advertiser would have to pay $5.00 for every 1,000 views of their ad.

Although an Impression measures the number of times a given ad was displayed on a site, it does not consider whether that ad was clicked on. Therefore, measuring the generated Impressions of a campaign is not an indicator of success or effectiveness. However, marketers can benefit from indirect competitive insight through Impression Share data on product groups, campaigns, keywords, and ad groups.

When dividing your campaign's total received Impressions by the total amount of Impressions it qualified for, you can determine the percentage of the total Impressions your ad campaigns are getting. For example, if you have 60% Impression share for a keyword, it means your competitors hold the other 40%, and if your Impression share increased, then the amount of times your competitors' ads are displayed would decrease..

Buyers will evaluate ad performance by comparing your CPM with industry standards to determine whether your ad strategy is effective, sustainable and whether or not they can improve performance further.

No matter which ad platform you are using, it will almost certainly display your CPM Trend.

Cost Per Click (CPC) is an alternative Metric to CPM that platforms such as Google AdWords and Facebook use to bill in Pay-Per-Click (PPC) marketing campaigns, based on how many times an advertisement is clicked. For instance, a website with a CPC rate of 20 cents that provides 1,000 click-throughs would charge $200 ($0.20 x 2,000).

The CPC Metric is commonly used by advertisers with a set daily budget. When that budget is hit, the ad is removed from the rotation for the rest of the billing period. The amount per click that an advertiser pays is affected by the campaign's Quality Score and is usually set either by a formula – Cost Per Impression (CPI) / Clickthrough Rate (CTR) – or through a bidding process.

Advertisers outplay competitors for ad positions with their bid, but end up paying the next-highest bid price. Therefore, regardless of predetermined budgets and maximum bids you are willing to pay for, the final cost depends heavily on other competitors in the CPC auction.

By analyzing a campaign's CPC in terms of value and cost, marketers are better equipped to calculate ROI and make marketing spend efficient. Focusing on identifying which clicks are cost-effective while spurring high-quality Traffic is crucial to maximizing the value of PPC advertising. The calculation is simple:

CPC ROI = Total Cost of Campaign ÷ Total Campaign Clicks

For example, if your ad gets two clicks, one costing $0.50 and one costing $0.20, the total cost is $0.70. Divide that by the total number of clicks (2), and you get an average CPC of $0.35.

Clickthrough Rate (CTR) %

Clickthrough Rate (CTR) is a key indicator for campaign performance, as it measures the percentage of individuals who see an online advertisement and subsequently click on it. CTR is used in a plethora of other mediums, such as the previously mentioned email and display advertising, and it determines a campaign's efficiency in capturing Users' attention. The higher the CTR, the more successful the ad has been in generating interest. CTRs can give advertisers insight into what works and what doesn't, and they can affect other Metrics like Quality Score. However, there is no benchmark CTR for measuring a campaign's success, since performance varies greatly by industry, budget spend, and many other variables. As internet Users are bombarded with hundreds of ads daily, they have become greatly desensitized towards them, and CTRs of just two Users per 1,000 views (0.2%) are now common. The equation for measuring CTR is the following:

CTR = Total Measured Ad Impressions ÷ Total Measured Clicks x 100

For example, if an ad was clicked 300 times after being served 30,000 times, you can find the CTR by dividing those numbers and multiplying the result by 100 to get the percentage ((300 / 30,000) x 100 = 1%).

Quality Score

Quality Score is a Metric used by Google, Yahoo, and Bing that influences ad rank and CPC. It is less straightforward than other easily measured Metrics, and therefore the most elusive performance indicator amongst advertisers.

Quality Score is an estimate of the quality of your ads, keywords, and landing pages. Google determines a campaign's Quality Score by using the expected CTR, landing page experience, ad relevance, and ad format. It is reported on a 1-10 scale, with higher Quality Scores (between 7-10) leading to lower Google Ads prices and better ad positions, while a low score leads to higher prices and poor ranking.

Recent Google changes in Quality Score reporting made it easier for advertisers to harness this Metric in Google Ads, in order to make smarter campaign decisions and get more from their marketing budget. The reports also started providing historical data about other key performance Metrics that Quality Score can affect, such as CPC and CPA.

You can simply find the 'keywords' tab of your Google, Bing or Yahoo Ads account to assess your current and historical scores for various keywords.

3.7.3 SOCIAL MEDIA MARKETING METRICS

Social Media Metrics refer to the performance of both paid and organic engagement with Users via Facebook, Instagram, Youtube, Twitter, Tik Tok, and the various other channels. Measuring the size and depth of the conversation taking place about your brand on social platforms will help you reach your marketing goals and generate more leads and sales.

Although tracking 'vanity' Metrics such as likes, shares, followers, and mentions is essential, buyers will go beyond the surface to determine if your social media strategies are effective. When a buyer asks you to talk data, the numbers in your report should cover Trends in the areas of Exposure, Reach, Engagement, and Social Share of Voice. Here are a few Social Media Metrics to track and measure:

SOCIAL MEDIA MARKETING METRICS

Audience Growth Rate

This Metric measures how fast your brand's followers, and therefore exposure, are increasing on social media. Notably, the emphasis here is not on the amount of net new followers, but on how quickly they were obtained and how that speed compares to your competitors'.

To calculate your (or your competitor's) Audience Growth Rate, you need to measure your new followers over a time period on each platform, divide that number by your total audience on each platform and multiply that by 100.

For instance, if last month, you gained 80 new Facebook followers and your total Facebook audience consists of 500 Users, then your Audience Growth Rate would be:

80/500 = 0.16 x 100 = 16%

Benchmarks for this Metric vary widely by industry and social media platform, but reporting on follower growth without the historical and competitive context would be just a futile exercise. By measuring your top competitors' Audience Growth Rate, you can highlight what the realistic speed for your industry is and determine if you are growing your audience effectively.

Post Reach

Post Reach refers to the dissemination of your content and the size of the audience that views it. Specifically, it indicates the number of people who have seen your content since it was posted on social media. Most, if not all, platforms will state an individual post's reach.

To calculate your Post Reach percentage, you need to divide the reach of a given post by the total number of followers on that platform and multiply that by 100. For example, if a Facebook post reached 150 people and your total followers are 500, then your Post Reach percentage would be:

150/500 = 0.3 x 100 = 30%

Achieving and maintaining a high Post Reach percentage is not only connected to the type of content, but also to the post's timing. Use data from your social networks, like Facebook's "When Your Fans Are Online" feature, to find the most favorable posting time and maximize your reach.

Potential Reach

Potential Reach refers to the number of people who could potentially and realistically view your post during a given period.

For example, when one of your followers shares your post with their network, then between 2% to 5% of their followers are included in that post's Potential Reach.

Tracking this Metric goes hand in hand with tracking your total number of brand mentions. Multiplying that number by the amount of followers of the account that mentioned you will give you your theoretical reach - in other words, the highest number of people who could theoretically see your brand mentions. Your Potential Reach is 2 - 5% of your theoretical reach.

Knowing and understanding your current and Potential Post Reach is something that every buyer would appreciate, as it is essential for expanding your audience and gauging your exposure progress.

If the social media platform doesn't calculate this for you, there are many social media tools that have this functionality built into their dashboard.

Average Engagement Rate

Engagement is about how much and in what way people are participating in the conversation about your brand.

Average Engagement Rate denotes how many engagement actions (shares, comments, likes) a post receives with regard to your total number of followers. A higher Engagement Rate means that your content resonates with your audience and captures their interest.

To track your Average Engagement Rate, add up the total shares, likes, and comments on a post, divide that number by the total of your followers and multiply by 100.

For example, if a Twitter post has generated 75 actions and your total followers are 800, then your Average Engagement Rate would be:

75/800 = 0.09 x 100 = 9%

Note that every platform has a different benchmark for this Metric, with Facebook and Twitter running on lower engagement rates of 0.5% to 1%, while Instagram and TikTok are known for relatively higher rates of up to 6% and 17% respectively.

Virality Rate

Virality Rate measures the amount of people who shared your post in proportion to its number of Impressions (Unique Views) during a specific period. If your social media goals are focused on spreading a message, then you would be aiming for a high Virality Rate, regardless of the amount of likes and comments. Think of it this way, a post with 500 likes and 10% virality is far better than a post with 10,000 likes and 0.5% virality.

Calculating your Virality Rate can be done by dividing the number of times a post was shared by the number of its Impressions and multiplying by 100. For example, if your post got 10 shares and 1000 Impressions, then your Virality Rate would be:

10/1000 = 0.01 x 100 = 1%

Ultimately, your Virality Rate will depend on the amount of followers you have, as well as the benchmark of each platform. For example, the median Virality Rate for Facebook pages is 1.92%, so a rate of +2.5% is considered strong.

Similar to the previous Metric, Amplification Rate shows how many of your followers are sharing your content via Twitter retweets, Facebook shares, Pinterest re-pins, and so on. The difference is that this Metric gives you the ratio of shares per post relative to the amount of total followers, as opposed to the number of Impressions.

Basically, a high Amplification Rate indicates that your followers are willing to share your posts, and associate themselves with your brand.

To calculate your Amplification Rate, add up the number of shares your post received during a particular time period, divide that by the number of overall followers, and multiply by 100.

For example, if your last Facebook post was shared 15 times and your follower base consists of 800 Users, then your Amplification Rate would be:

15/800 = 0.018 x 100 = 1.8%

Bottomline, in the eyes of the buyer, a higher Amplification Rate means a stronger follower base and higher chances of turning leads into converting customers.

Social Share of Voice (SSoV)

A brand's Social Share of Voice (SSoV) is the market share equivalent of the social media world. How much space do your posts occupy out of the total percentage of discussions about your industry or a specific topic?

Social Share of Voice helps determine your brand's exposure and position in the industry based on social media conversation. Essentially, SSoV is a competitor analysis regarding your brand's visibility and relevance in the market, based on how many mentions - direct ('@Exitplanr') or indirect ('Exitplanr') - your brand is getting compared to your competition.

To calculate your SSoV, first measure any direct and indirect mentions your brand received across your social platforms within a particular period. Then estimate your competitors' mentions for the same time period and calculate the total industry mentions by adding the two numbers. Divide your mentions by the grand total and multiply by 100.

This is the formula you can follow to track this Metric:

$$\text{SSoV} = \text{Your Mentions} \div \text{Total Mentions} \times 100$$

By measuring and comparing your SSoV to your competitors', you will have an idea of where you stand and what actions you can take so that the conversation gravitates towards your brand. The bigger the percentage of your SSoV, the more popular you will be among your audience, potential customers, and, of course, Buyers.

3.7.4 CONTENT MARKETING METRICS

Content Marketing is the creation, distribution, and publishing of content for a targeted online audience. This content may not explicitly promote your brand, but the intent is to stimulate your audience's interest in your product or services by using well-organized content strategies. To measure the success and performance of your digital content, you need clearly defined targets and a continuous analysis of the results. Let's have a look at some major Content Marketing Metrics to track:

Pages Per Session

This Metric gives you the average number of pages visited by your Users during a session. Basically, it shows you how 'sticky' your site is, so naturally, you should be aiming for a high number. The more valuable and helpful your content is, the more motivated your visitors will be to explore other pages and dive deeper into your website.

To monitor Pages Per Session, simply go to Google Analytics > Acquisition > Overview

Page Depth

Page Depth gives you the average number of your website's pages that Users visit after your landing page. It is a good indicator of your overall content's engagement and interlinking quality. A high Page Depth number is essential if your Content Marketing goals include building a readership and directing its attention towards your 'money' pages.

Average Dwell Time

Put simply, Average Dwell Time is the time a User spends on evaluating if your content will provide the information they need after clicking on your page from the Google search results. If it doesn't, they'll go back to the Search Engine Results Page (SERP). But if the dwell time on your site is long, Google will understand that your content serves the purposes of this particular search and will rank you higher on the SERP.

While there is no particular Google Analytics Metric or formula to track Average Dwell Time, you can use other Metrics and areas as guiding indicators:

- Aim to increase your Time On Page
- Aim to prolong your Session Duration
- Aim to decrease your Bounce Rate
- Ensure your Website Loading Speed is fast
- Ensure your website's navigation tools provide a good user experience

Average Time On Page

Another Metric you should be trying to keep high is your Average Time On Page, or how much time a visitor spends on your webpage or post. It is a good indicator of how engaging and digestible your content is from top to bottom. Most posts nowadays state their average reading time (e.g. '5 min read'), given that most people will devote between five to seven minutes to reading a post. Google Analytics will give you the Average Time On Page for individual pages or posts on your website, and the general Trend of your pages altogether.

Comments & Shares

If you are distributing your website content through social media platforms, comments and shares are the best indicator of quality content that has the potential to go viral. Shares expand your content's reach, increase your follower base, and boost your brand authority.

On the other end, comments on your blogs shed light on the topics that are conversation starters and help you rank higher on SERP, thus driving more organic Traffic to your website. Tracking your blog post comments is easily done in most platforms like WordPress or Joomla, or via services like Commentful and Disqus.

Content Marketing ROI

The effectiveness of your Content Marketing strategy in generating a profit will be ultimately determined by your Content Marketing ROI. Here is the calculation formula:

(Content Campaign Revenue – Cost of Expenses) – Content Campaign Cost

For example, if your Content Marketing efforts over the past six months have generated a revenue of $10,000 and the expenses to deliver your product/service cost $3,000, then your profit is $7,000. At this point, as long as the cost of your content campaign is less than $7,000, you have made money. Let's say your campaign cost $2,000, then your Content Marketing ROI would be $5,000.

If you are making a profit from your Content Marketing efforts, then you should either continue or invest more in the chosen activities. If you are losing money or breaking even, then it might be time to consider changing your strategy.

All things being equal, Content Marketing takes time to bear fruit. It usually takes between six to 12 months to see a positive ROI from Content Marketing efforts, depending on your network, skills, and ability to grow your business.

Buyers will certainly want to ensure that your company's Content Marketing brings noteworthy results, so allow yourself at least six months to generate a good ROI for your reports.

3.7.5 SEARCH MARKETING METRICS

Search Marketing refers to the incorporation of SEO tactics in online content and site architecture in order to increase a website's visibility and achieve a higher ranking in SERPs. Consequently, your Search Marketing Metrics reflect how you work the search algorithms on search engines to your advantage.

The competition to land the top spots on a search page is fierce, and you need every trick up your sleeve to be able to rise in the ranks. Organic Traffic and Referral Traffic are the most common Metrics to be tracking, but to dive a bit deeper into your SEO effectiveness, you need to also consider the following:

SEARCH MARKETING METRICS

Domain Authority

Also known as Domain Rating, Domain Authority (DA) measures how strong, authoritative, or 'famous' your website is compared to other sites. While it is a Metric with a very wide scope, it is used as an index by many content marketers to determine how fast a content piece will get indexed and ranked, as well as its likelihood to rank higher than the competition.

The factors that largely determine a website's DA are the number and quality of backlinks that link to your website's domain, along with your domain's age and your website's size. Having a big number of backlinks from domains that have a high DA themselves boosts the Domain Authority of your website, as opposed to having few and low-quality links.

Naturally, established brands and older domains tend to have higher DA, thanks to the necessary quality and quantity of backlinks acquired due to their longevity. That said, if a website is not regularly maintained in terms of SEO and fresh content, the domain will eventually fall into disrepair, and lose its DA.

It takes time to establish your DA, but to access and track it easily from the beginning, you need to invest in tools like Moz or Ahrefs.

Domain Authority scores in both Moz and Ahrefs are on a 100-point scale, with 100 being the best. However, the reality is that there is no perfect DA score because Domain Authority is a comparative Metric. Therefore, a good score would depend on your direct competition of similar Business Size and scale, including companies that rank for the same keywords you do.

There are a number of platforms, including Moz, AHRefs and SEMRush that will display current and historical data on your Domain Authority.

Link Profile

Link Profile is the makeup of external links, known as backlinks, that your domain receives from other websites, either for citing a reference from your content or backing up facts and statistics. Although any backlink would be considered a boost, you need to monitor and ensure that the majority of those links come from relevant websites with high DA.

Too many toxic and spammy links from questionable or irrelevant sources with low DA could, in fact, hurt your Search Rankings and reduce your website's authority. Seeing as how your Link Profile accounts for the vast majority of your website's ranking as per Google's algorithm, you might want to consider disavowing such links. Since there is no benchmark for a good Link Profile, the strategy for working with backlinks needs to be selected individually for each business.

To professionally access, filter, and monitor your backlinks, you will need SEO tools like Moz, SEMrush or Ahrefs.

Organic Traffic Value

Organic Traffic Value is the estimated amount of money you would be paying for Traffic from all the keywords your website is ranking for if you pay via Google's Pay-Per-Click (PPC) instead of trying to rank for them organically.

Put simply, this Metric tells you how much money you've saved from buying Paid Traffic by ranking for keywords organically and how valuable your domain's keyword profile is. The higher the Organic Traffic Value, the better - not only in terms of cost savings, but also in terms of commercial intent.

Informational keywords like 'best SEO Metrics for 2021' tend to have lower Traffic value (CPC) than certain 'punchy' keywords with higher Traffic value, such as 'top SEO Metrics'. Ideally, you should aim to have a good mix of both high-search, low-volume Traffic value, and low-search, high-volume Traffic keywords in your content campaign.

There are several formulas to calculate your monthly Organic Traffic Value, but the best way to accurately track and access it is by using tools like Ahrefs or SEMrush.

Organic Keyword Ranking

Tracking the number of Organic Keywords that your website and content ranks for, as well as their individual rankings in Google's top 10, is essential for determining your SEO success. The more organic keywords you have in your website, the better the chances of ranking higher in search engines and, therefore, generating higher search engine Traffic. It is equally important to invest in organic keyword placement in order to place selected keywords at places where search engines pay more attention to when examining website content. Ideally, you should be aiming for your domain to rank for 100 to 1,000 keywords relevant to your industry.

To access, track, and monitor your organic keywords, you will need to invest in SEO tools like Ahrefs or SEMrush. As Google algorithms change often, setting up alerts with such tools is highly recommended.

We haven't touched on every marketing channel (public relations, affiliate marketing, online community/forums, to name a few) nor have we even gotten close to covering the full list of performance Metrics that can be used to assess a business' health and trajectory.

That said, you should have a pretty good sense for what Metrics you should be tracking in your business. Keep in mind that you should identify the key Metrics that are most important to your particular business. By closely monitoring the right Metrics, you can make adjustments in your business and measure their impact. In all likelihood, you will find ways to improve the overall performance of your business and therefore, its value over time.

ACTIVITY 3

Gauge Your Performance

Every aspect of your business' performance will create (a) Upwards Pressure, (b) Downward Pressure, or (c) Neutral Pressure (aka no pressure) on your Earnings Multiplier. As you will intuitively know, strong performance creates Upward Pressure, weak performance creates Downward Pressure, some aspects of your business will have a greater impact than others, and some won't have any impact at all. With that said, I want you to select up to three metrics for each performance category and measure three things:

1. Pressure: determine whether this metric creates ↑ Upward, ↓ Downward or ~ Neutral pressure on the Multiplier.

2. Impact: score the likely impact this pressure will have on your Multiplier out of 3 (1 or -1 = small impact, 2 or -2 = big impact, 3 or -3 = huge impact)

3. Calculate the total pressure applied to your Multiplier

   a. Sum of Upward Pressure impact points (e.g. 5)

   b. Sum of Downward Pressure impact points (e.g -3)

   c. Subtract Downward Pressure impact points from Upward Pressure impact points (5-3 = 2)

If you're feeling unsure about how a particular aspect of your performance will impact your Multiplier, refer to the content above, talk to a friend, or an advisor, and of course there's always Google.

METRIC	PRESSURE	IMPACT
FINANCIAL PERFORMANCE		
1. *E.g. Revenue Trend or ARR / MRR Trend (just pick one)*	*↑ Upward Pressure*	*2*
2. Earnings Trend		
3. Gross Profit Trend		
WEB TRAFFIC PERFORMANCE		
1.		
2.		
3.		
CUSTOMER PERFORMANCE		
1.		
2.		
3.		
MARKETING PERFORMANCE		
1.		
2.		
3.		
	TOTAL PRESSURE =	

KEY TAKEAWAYS

PERFORMANCE GAUGE

- Business Performance is the most impactful Pressure Gauge because it helps Buyers determine the time, effort, and resources required to recoup their Initial Investment, as well as maintaining or growing its value in the future.

- There are three modes of performance; current performance, past performance and future performance.

- Current performance typically refers to Trailing 12 Months (TTM) of business. However, if your business is less than a year old or is experiencing rapid growth or decline, Buyers will use Trailing Six Months (T6M) and Trailing Three Months (T3M) to measure current performance.

- Past performance refers to historical performance in years gone by and is analyzed and compared with Current performance to establish the performance Trend of your business.

- Future performance can only be speculative because the future is the future – *it hasn't happened yet*. Nevertheless, Buyers forecast the future performance of a business by analyzing Trends in key performance Metrics.

- Buyers will look to analyze Trends in four key areas; financial performance, web traffic performance, customer performance and marketing performance.

- Financial Performance acts as an umbrella and a *catch-all* for all the performance Metrics because every other Metric influences how a business performs financially in one way or another. Key Metrics include Revenue Trend, gross profit %, Earnings Trend, etc.)

- Web Traffic Performance provides you (as well as prospective buyers) with vital information about how people arrive on your site and how they engage with its content. Key Metrics include bounce rate Trend, sessions Trend, and session duration Trend.

- While Traffic performance Metrics tell us about how people interact with your website, Customer Performance Metrics tell us about how customers are transacting with your business. Key Metrics include Repeat Customer Rate %, Churn Rate, Customer Lifetime Value, and LTV:CAC Ratio.

- Marketing Performance Metrics allow us to track and measure the effectiveness of particular marketing initiatives, activities and campaigns. Key Metrics include Email Open Rate, Advertising ROI, and Link Profile.

GAUGING SUSTAINABILITY

4

4. GAUGING SUSTAINABILITY

Sustainability relates to the overall health of a business. In other words, it considers the likelihood of sustaining current business performance in the future. This is predominantly determined by evaluating the quality of your product or service offering, how you acquire and retain customers, the *true* value of your average customer, as well as its resilience to changing market conditions. Sustainability can create significant pressure in both directions too, albeit slightly more on the negative side.

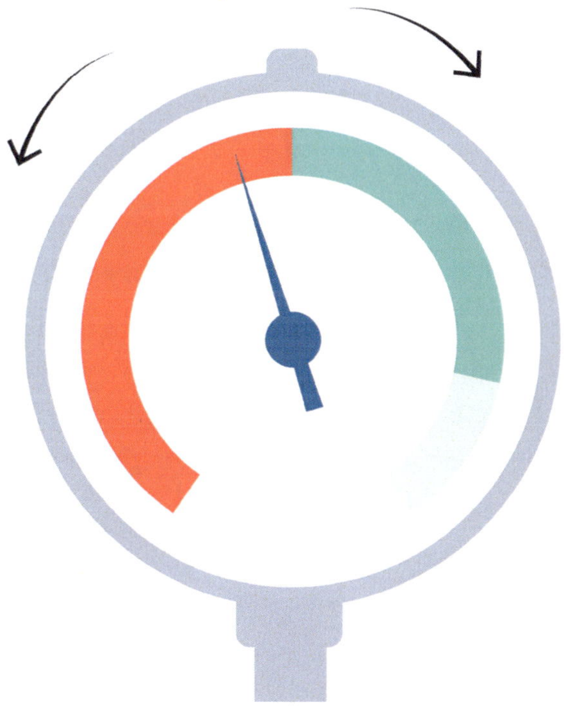

In this Chapter, we explore how the following key factors impact the Sustainability and the value of your business:

- Product and Service Offering
- Market Resilience
- Customer Channels
- Channel Diversity
- Customer Conversion
- Customer Retention and Churn
- Customer Value

4.1 PRODUCT AND SERVICE OFFERING

The quality of your product and service offering forms the foundation of your entire business and has a major influence on its ability to sustain performance over time. In today's world, where competitor offerings are just a click away, the strength of your offering is more important than ever before.

If your offering leaves customers unsatisfied, then the likelihood of acquiring repeat business or new customers becomes less and less as time goes on. On the other hand, the stronger your products and services are, the greater customer satisfaction and thus loyalty your brand will have. Buyers are generally willing to pay a higher price for a business with a strong offering and loyal customer base, because they are generally more sustainable (and scalable). The easiest way to capture the quality of a business' offering is to establish how satisfied your customer base is. That is to say:

Product & Service Quality = Customer Satisfaction

This means we can use the same Traffic and Customer Performance Metrics mentioned in 3.5

and 3.6 to evaluate your offering and identify ways you can improve it.

Review sites are an easy way for buyers to get a sense for how customers rate the products and services that you offer. Reviews also have a strong influence on future customers who are deciding whether or not to shop with you. Potential customers will often search reviews on Google, Trust Pilot, Rip Off Report and various niche-specific forums and websites before making a purchase decision. If you sell through Third-party platforms like Amazon, Etsy or Ebay, your customer rating will largely determine the market's perception of your offering and therefore brand.

If you discover negative reviews, try to put your ego aside and consider them objectively. Ask yourself whether the customer makes a valid suggestion on how your offering could be improved.

After all, as Bill Gates famously said, "*Your most unhappy customers are your biggest source of learning*." If you feel like the reviews are unfair and having a damaging effect on acquiring new customers or selling your business, you may want to consider any of the following brand reputation management tactics:

- Encouraging customers who had a positive experience to write reviews
- Responding to customers who leave negative reviews to seek a resolution
- Flagging fake reviews and requesting their removal
- Enlisting legal help in seeking the removal of defamatory content
- Creating a company profile on a review platform that guarantees authenticity of its reviews through blockchain technology, like Revain.org.

Other customer Metrics such as Net Promoter Score, Repeat Customer Rate, Churn Rate, Refund Rate, and so on, are all useful Metrics when determining the quality and strength of a business' offering, which we will examine further when we look at Customer Retention in 4.6.

4.2 MARKET RESILIENCE

Market Resilience is measured by a business' ability to sustain performance during economic downturns, market disruptions and other adversities that a business will inevitably endure along the way. Obviously, the quality of your product and service offering will influence your resilience to adverse market conditions and there are things you can do to improve your Market Resilience and Sustainability over time.

That said, there are some industries and Business Models that are inherently more resilient than others. In the event of an economic downturn, an SaaS business providing hosting services would usually fare a lot better than a Shopify store selling jewelry. This is because consumers generally purchase jewelry with their disposable income, whereas business owners pay their hosting bills to keep their online businesses...well, *online*!

RESILIENCE

The COVID-19 pandemic-induced global recession

is the most recent example of such a resilience test. While many online businesses celebrated unprecedented growth through the explosion of online transactions driven by physical distancing requirements, there were also many online businesses that have suffered greatly. Some sectors, like the travel industry, have been completely annihilated.

Resilience does not only relate to how inherently durable the business is but also its ability to respond and recover to adverse conditions. Businesses that are more dynamic are able to dodge bullets or clench opportunities easier than their slow and cumbersome counterparts. Dynamism is a tricky thing to measure because it is predominantly determined by the Leadership and Culture of a business (9.13).

Is your business on-trend or evergreen?

Another factor that should be considered is whether or not your business is *on-trend* or *evergreen*. As you well know, market demand is in constant flux and is influenced in myriad ways, be it from economic collapse, a publicity stunt or changes in season. The release of popular Netflix Series 'The Queen's Gambit' in 2020 sent chess set sales skyrocketing across the globe. You can bet Chess.com is enjoying their hockey stick growth Trend, too!

So, is Chess.com a trending or evergreen business? Well, I would argue that Chess.com is an evergreen business that is currently on-trend. Unsurprisingly, there is nothing more enticing to a buyer than a trending evergreen business, because they can ride the gravy train while it's trending and sleep soundly at night, knowing there will be strong market

IS YOUR BUSINESS ON-TREND OR EVERGREEN

Viral or Trending	Evergreen
Viral or Trending businesses are characterized by the market's demand for their product, which is typically tied to a specific event or time period that is either short-lived or expected to drop off significantly in the future. Former US President Donald Trump was the catalyst for hundreds of new retail products designed to mock or celebrate the public figure. Naturally, as his prevalence in the media fades, so will the demand for Trump piñatas and T-shirts alike. Similarly, the pandemic gave birth to many online businesses selling face masks and antiseptic products. If it is no longer mandatory to wear masks in public, demand will drop significantly and so will the profitability of these businesses.	Evergreen businesses stay relevant and in high demand over long periods of time, presenting buyers with potential for long-term Profit and low-risk investment. Like chess, there are some markets and industries where there will always be strong demand. For instance, businesses operating in health, food, sport, and arts sectors will most likely be considered evergreen. Unless people collectively stop caring about their health, what they eat, their sports teams and their favorite artists, products and services in this niche will live on long after you and I are six feet under.

demand long after the hype dies down. Why do I say this with such confidence? Because early forms of chess were invented in India in the 7th Century AD, and it has been growing in popularity around the world ever since. Plus, any data scientist will tell you that online gaming is only going to increase in popularity. So chess + online = evergreen - capish?

So, do all Viral or Trending businesses make bad acquisitions? Absolutely not. In fact, there are a group of buyers (albeit small) out there that are specifically looking for these types of businesses. Plus, businesses like Chess.com might be enjoying the best of both worlds. Another important consideration is the distinction between viral Trends and *emerging markets*.

An Emerging Market is a new sector that rapidly gains popularity and is expected to continue expanding over a longer period of time. Blockchain technology is an excellent example of an Emerging Market that is almost certainly here to stay. Despite currently being used mostly in the volatile cryptocurrency sector, there are several benefits that blockchain can offer to different industries that cement its position and propel its distribution. Those include enhanced traceability, increased accountability, greater security, and improved performance - market needs that will continue to be addressed as we move forward into the digital era.

Contrarily, a few years ago, we saw the inexplicable demand for fidget spinners rise and fall within months, perfectly exemplifying a viral product with a short shelf life. The gadget gained immense popularity amongst teenagers in December 2016, mostly due to increased social media share and promotion. With no existing patent or licensing fees to pay, various firms in China started manufacturing spinners in huge quantities, and almost every shop was able to stock the unbranded goods from wherever they could find them to satisfy the market demand. However, kids quickly moved on, and by June 2017, fidget spinners had lost their prominence and were dismissed as a toy fad.

So, take a step back from your business and without bias, ask yourself this simple question: will market demand *die, slow, stagnate or grow?*

4.3 CUSTOMER CHANNELS

Customer Channels (or Customer Acquisition Channels) refer to the different ways a customer first engages with your brand. Did they meet you at a conference or find you on the first page of Google Search? Or perhaps your brand appeared on their social media news feed?

In other words, your Customer Channels are a culmination of the sales, marketing and business development activities that you use to attract potential leads and convert them into paying customers.

Buyers will analyze each of your Customer Acquisition Channels to determine whether or not they are sustainable, as well as the time and resources that would be required to sustain or grow the customer base under their ownership. Buyers and valuers alike will want to know the answers to questions like these:

> *"Is the business reliant on a single Customer Channel?"*

"What is the customer Conversion Rate?"

"What is the Customer Retention Rate?"

"What is the average cost of acquiring a customer?"

"What is the average Customer Lifetime Value?"

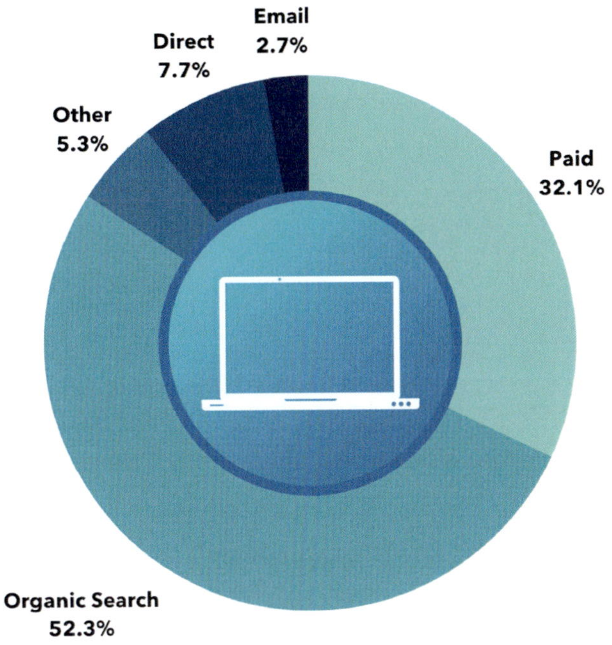

4.4 CHANNEL DIVERSITY

Channel Diversity relates to the mix of channels used to acquire new customers. A business that relies too heavily on a single Customer Channel is usually considered a lot riskier than a business acquiring customers through multiple channels. So if the majority of your customers stem from a single channel, you may wish to focus your efforts on diversifying your marketing mix and customer acquisition strategies. Customer Channels can be separated into three distinct categories:

- Website Traffic
- Third-Party Platform
- Direct/Offline

4.4.1 WEBSITE TRAFFIC SOURCES

Like all online businesses, most (if not all) transactions flow through your website, which is why analyzing website Traffic sources is a quick and easy way to evaluate the Sustainability of a business. Google Analytics categorizes Traffic sources into the following categories:

Direct Traffic

You will typically see Buyers begin to raise concerns when Direct Traffic is above 30%. Direct Traffic can be a valuable channel when associated with strong brand recognition, and a high volume of returning visitors via type-in Traffic or bookmarks. However, if you have a young, unestablished brand with no reasonable explanation for the high volumes of Direct Traffic, you should investigate further. This is because unexplained Direct Traffic - otherwise known as *'Dark Traffic'* - can be the result of Google Analytics installation errors, or worse, *bot Traffic*, which can make Buyers apprehensive about the legitimacy and Sustainability of this Traffic source.

Organic Search Traffic

Organic Search Traffic is generated when people click on your organic listing on search engines such as Google and Bing. This is generally considered desirable traffic because it is often made up of highly targeted visitors who have a specific intent and therefore greater likelihood of conversion. However, Google and other search engines are constantly updating their search algorithm, and even a slight adjustment could result in a significant drop in Traffic volume to your website. For this reason, if more than 60% of your total Traffic stems from Organic Search, it is worth looking into diversifying your Traffic channels.

Referral Traffic

It depends on the quality and diversity of the referring links. Referral Traffic originates from a user clicking on your link from another website, excluding Traffic tagged from other major channels, such as Social or Organic Search. The quality of the referring link is of utmost importance because good links can improve your visibility in search and bad links can result in penalties. Referral Traffic is valuable when it originates from organically generated links found on the websites of popular, trustworthy sites like Forbes Magazine or CNN.

However, if the Referral Traffic is generated from untrustworthy, spammy websites then the Traffic source is considerably less sustainable. Apart from the imminent risk of being penalized in search engines, spammy links are also much more likely to be removed than an article posted on CNN. The other factor Buyers will consider is the diversity of your Link Profile. If a backlink from CNN generates 30% of your Traffic volume, it means your business is highly dependent on that single link. Unsurprisingly, Buyers would much prefer your Referral Traffic to be the accumulation of dozens of links from authority websites like CNN.

Email Traffic

Email Traffic is a highly valued Customer Channel and the exception to the rule because unlike other Traffic sources, it isn't dependent on a third party. That is to say that this Traffic source cannot be adversely impacted by the removal of a link or a changing algorithm. As long as your email subscribers can voluntarily opt in and opt out at their choosing, there isn't really such a thing as too much Email Traffic. The only legitimate criticism one can make is that you're leaving easy money on the table if email marketing is the only channel in which you're acquiring customers. However, if your Email Traffic is largely generated through unsolicited spam email campaigns, buyers will view this Traffic source as far less sustainable and will likely reduce your Valuation considerably. If Email Traffic is an important Traffic source for your business, Buyers will also analyze the Metrics mentioned in 3.7.1 related to customer engagement. To ensure strong email performance, make sure your email lists are regularly scrubbed of any inactive subscribers.

Social Media Traffic

You will generally get a lot of questions when Social Media Traffic accounts for more than half of the total Traffic sources. Social Media Traffic is represented by website visitors acquired through social platforms such as Facebook, Instagram, Twitter, Youtube, and LinkedIn. While recognized as a legitimate Traffic source, many business owners fail to separate Organic Social Media Traffic from Paid Social Media Traffic. If this is an issue for your business, shift to creating custom-tagged URLs, which will allow you (and potential Buyers) to better visualize Paid vs. Organic Social Media Traffic in Google Analytics. Despite being the most widely used social media platform, Facebook's News Feed algorithm is considered highly volatile and therefore susceptible to fast and unexpected change. That being said, as social media platforms continue to mature and stabilize, it is likely that Organic Social Media Traffic will be considered just as strong as Organic Search Traffic in the near future.

Paid Search Traffic

It depends on your advertising approach, but generally speaking, buyers begin to get uncomfortable when Paid Search exceeds 40% of total Traffic sources. Paid Search, also known as PPC, is where you pay to appear on the first page of a search engine's search results for certain keywords. Provided your business has consistently achieved great results with Paid Search and your formula is transferable under new ownership, your business will be considered somewhat sustainable. However, some Buyers will be wary if your business is wholly dependent on Paid Search, because keywords may become more expensive in the future, reducing your ROI on ad spend.

Furthermore, if your business employs an arbitrage-style Paid Search strategy by bidding on low-cost, irrelevant keywords to drive Traffic to your website and generate income through display advertising, then you are likely to see your Valuation shrink considerably, due to the high-risk, unsustainable nature of the advertising arbitrage model.

Display Advertising Traffic

It is common for Buyers raise concerns about the over-concentration of Display Advertising Traffic when it accounts for more than 40% of total Traffic. Display Advertising Traffic is acquired through display ad networks, such as AdWords, AdRoll, etc. Paid advertising through ad networks can be very attractive, because it is measurable and, in some cases, extremely scalable. Of course, the main risk associated with any paid advertising is the fluctuating ROI. The prices of ad clicks are always changing, and if the competition in your niche gets stronger, the price is likely to rise and your ROI margin percentage is likely to drop.

While the above definitions may seem simple, it is important to remember that Google Analytics assigns Traffic to channels based on the source and/or medium. This is another reason why it is so important to correctly tag your campaigns to ensure data reliability.

While analyzing a website's source of Traffic is extremely effective in determining the Sustainability of various Customer Channels, it does not cover every Customer Channel. Customers may transact with your business over the phone, via email, or on Third-Party Platforms like Amazon or Google Play, and so on.

4.4.2 THIRD-PARTY PLATFORMS

Just like Google Analytics provides invaluable website Traffic data, Third-Party Platforms have their own Metrics that can help you, valuers and potential buyers assess the Sustainability of a particular customer channel.

If you sell products via Fulfillment by Amazon (FBA), your overall seller rating is scored out of 100 and is determined by Seller Feedback, and *Metrics like Order Defect Rate, Late Dispatch Rate, Contact Response Time*. A Seller Feedback rating above 85 indicates that your customers are happy, giving Buyers confidence that this particular channel is likely to continue converting customers. Conversely, Amazon accounts with a poor Seller Feedback rating will find it increasingly difficult to acquire customers through this channel, and in extreme cases, run the risk of being suspended or terminated.

If you sell products on eBay, the Metrics and benchmarks you should track can be found in the marketplace's reporting features: Seller Hub and Seller Standards Dashboard. The first includes *Sales Conversion Rate, Average Seller Rating* and other price competitiveness Metrics. The Seller Standards Dashboard includes KPIs for each Merchant, including *Late Shipment Rate, Transaction Defect Rate, and overall Seller Level*. The average Seller Rating on Seller Hub is above 98%, so adhering to or exceeding this high benchmark gives Buyers the impression of a well-performing eBay business that is likely to sustain its current performance. Contrarily, a lower Seller Rating can discourage old and new buyers from purchasing your items, thus damaging your business' image with prospective buyers.

Although most Etsy shop owners integrate their Etsy account with Google Analytics, there are still a good amount of Metrics and statistics that the platform provides on Traffic, Listings, and Customers. With the Etsy Stats and Pattern Metrics, you can monitor your shop's overall performance, your Traffic sources, and how shoppers are engaging with your listings. Financial stats, particularly Conversion Rate and Revenue, can be compared to previous years to establish how they are trending. An increasing number of visitors, and an upward trending Revenue and Conversion Rate indicate sustainable growth, and will inspire more confidence in Buyers interested in purchasing your Etsy shop.

Apple provides an extensive analytics platform for measuring your app's performance. The App Analytics provides unique insights with useful Metrics such as Conversion Rate, Retention Rate, Sales per Paying Users, and reports on how your sales are trending over time. Developers are required to follow strict guidelines on privacy, design, and Business Models in order to retain user trust. Apple automated systems and human experts carefully review each app on a regular basis to ensure that a high standard of technical performance, security and content is maintained. Hence, data on your App Store Optimization and strong performance will demonstrate increased likelihood of continued success, and strengthen growth prospects amongst Buyers.

Similarly, Google Play offers reports and statistics on the Play Console platform to help you monitor and track key Metrics, Trends, and data. Those include User Acquisitions, Returning Users, Average revenue per Monthly Active User, as well as Average Rating. Google Play has a vast list of policies, benchmarks and technical requirements that Android developers are expected to abide by in order to maintain and constantly improve their app's performance, stability, and size. Apps with higher Metrics get better promotability, thus ranking higher in Google Play Store searches. They also have higher chances of being included in the 'New & Updated' and 'Editor's Choice' collections on Google Play, as well as being nominated in the

Google Play Awards. Therefore, a well-performing Google Play account indicates satisfied Users and good overall quality level that would please any potential Buyer.

4.4.3 OFFLINE (DIRECT) CUSTOMER CHANNELS

What if some of your customers don't transact via your website or a Third-Party Platform? How do you measure the Sustainability of those less tangible Customer Channels? These questions are especially poignant for wholesalers, enterprise software providers, or any company that sells products and services through Business-to-Business (B2B) and Business-to-Government (B2G) channels. Such businesses typically rely less on digital marketing, and more so on relationship building. Networking, direct sales outreach, strategic partnerships, organic (word of mouth) referrals, and partner referrals are examples of direct/offline Customer Channels that are not fully captured by Google Analytics nor Third-Party Platforms.

For instance, a previous customer may recommend your product to a friend over coffee and introduce them to you directly by email. Similarly, they might give you a call or ask to meet you in person. All of these events can be captured, analyzed and monitored through a Customer Relationship Management (CRM) system. If your business acquires customers through direct or offline channels and doesn't already utilize the benefits of a CRM, it is strongly recommended that you add this as a priority task on your to-do list once you have completed this guide.

Measuring offline marketing with a proficient CRM program can be crucial for successfully tracking lead management, sales journey, customer satisfaction, conversions, and retention rate. Using a comprehensive CRM program also allows you to store all client information in one place, so that you can tailor conversations and enhance each interaction. Businesses can fully track their performance by integrating their direct marketing channels into a CRM software, and correlate online and offline marketing efforts to retarget customers.

Let's take a look at five ways you can track offline and direct marketing efforts by using CRM solutions:

Unique Discount Code

CRM software can help track unique discount codes on direct mail and print ads by using analytics for trailing and measuring escalation, customer profiling and predictive modeling. Some platforms can even generate specific discount codes, which can be directly integrated into the software and provide insights on each customer's response to the outreach.

Customized landing page

Redirecting offline Traffic to a custom landing page is a common way of tracking offline campaigns. Offline materials, such as brochures, flyers, and billboards contain a promotional URL or QR code that prompts leads to the landing page, where the CRM monitors the number of page visits.

Tracking direct mail

Businesses often automate direct mail marketing using CRM tools, and add a digital tie-in to every email, be it in the form of QR code, discount/ coupon code, or landing page. This way, the CRM software tracks and collects data on the response rate the direct mail campaign is garnering.

Tracking cold calls

Collecting sufficient information through cold calls and chat lines can be time consuming. Hence, businesses that practice cold calling usually integrate unique phone numbers on their CRM, allowing the calls to be synchronized with the software. This gives instant access to the client's profile, so that reps know who they are talking to, and can easily add or update their data, and track performance. Some CRM programs even allow businesses to import a client/cold-call database from sources such as CSV, XLSX, vCard files, or other third-party apps such as LinkedIn, Outlook, Mac Address Book, and Google Contacts. In addition, unique phone numbers can be included on various ads, in order to determine which sources are driving conversions.

Event tracking

In the case of offline events, CRM software can be used to create a campaign for driving offline audiences online in order to track and retarget them. These campaigns usually involve a tracking URL on print materials that links to the QR code for a landing page integrated into the CRM.

When customers visit that landing page, the data is acquired by the software, and can be used to retarget niche customers in digital campaigns. When it comes to quantifying your offline customer relationships and assessing your direct marketing efforts, the Metrics available in your CRM are essential for attaining success.

Tracking these data points will help you determine what activities are productive, benchmark and optimize your campaigns, as well as predict revenue and ROI. Of the six 'must-track' CRM Metrics pointing to growth, there are three we have already discussed at length in the previous 3.6: Customer Acquisition Cost (CAC), Customer Lifetime Value (CLV), and Net Promoter Score (NPS). However, there are three more CRM Metrics that deserve your attention:

Length of Sales Cycle: This Metric refers to the average time it takes to convert a lead. Your closing speed data helps you determine touchpoints where leads are sinking, and establish a timeline for mid-funnel engagement to accelerate your sales cycle. This way, the CRM software makes your sales process more efficient, and helps you optimize the velocity of your sales pipeline - meaning you can sell more in less time.

Upsell Rate: Upselling is the process of convincing a customer to spend more by buying an upgraded or premium version of what they had originally planned to purchase. For example, if one in every five customers upgrades their purchase of your product/service, your upsell rate is 20%. Your CRM can help increase your upsell rate by finding upsell Trend predictors in your customer database. Put simply, it helps you predict which leads are most likely to spend more on additional products or upgrades so that you know which groups to target.

Campaign Performance: In most CRM programs, this Metric comes in the form of a report that gives you the revenue generated from each marketing campaign. This is especially important for eCommerce businesses that look to test and improve their marketing strategies. A good CRM helps you break down how much you actually make from each campaign, and determine how many people you convinced to buy from you. Identifying what resonates with your customers according to their behavior and preferences is essential in order to send the right messages to the right people.

By now you should understand the importance of having multiple Customer Channels and how the Sustainability of each primary Customer Channel is evaluated.

4.5 CHANNEL CONVERSION

While Customer Acquisition Channels provide integral insight into how potential customers engage with your brand, it is doubly important to establish which channels are converting these leads into paying customers.

It is also important to note that a one-time customer is nowhere near as valuable as a repeat customer, or even better - *a serial customer*. So just because Organic Search Traffic is generating the most amount of visits to your website every day doesn't mean it is the most valuable Customer Channel. In fact, Organic Search Traffic might only produce a handful of one-time customers, whereas customers acquired through Referral Traffic may convert hundreds of serial repeat customers. Therefore, in order to properly evaluate the performance and Sustainability of a Customer Channel, you must study its Conversion Rate.

As we explained in 3.7, Conversion Rate is the percentage of potential customers that convert into paying customers by making a purchase, signing up for a subscription, upgrading their service, and so on. If you set up your tracking right, most online advertising and analytics platforms can directly display your Conversion Rate in their interface. You can monitor not only your overall Conversion data, but also the Conversion Rate of different Customer Acquisition Channels, marketing campaigns, individual ads, and more.

Although it is easy to assume that a high Conversion Rate is enough to convince buyers, what they will also look to evaluate is the Sustainability of your customer Conversion tactics. Businesses employ a plethora of tactics to convert their leads into paying customers, some of which

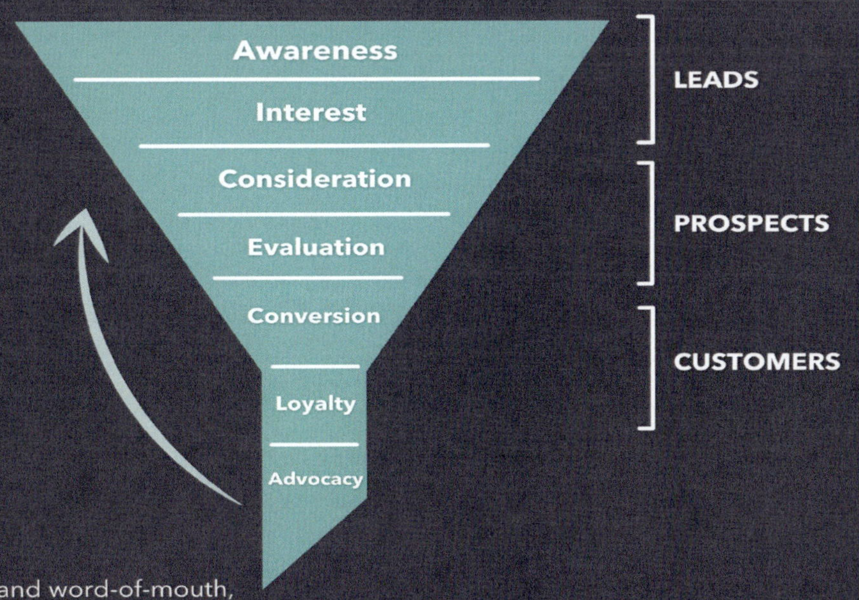

Through advocacy and word-of-mouth, converted customers are able to send new leads to the top of the funnel for you.

are less sustainable than others, and produce short-term gain dwarfed by longer-term losses. For example, a business that is constantly converting by running flash sales and large discounts on its products or services will lose points with buyers and may see a dip in value.

While such tactics can boost Conversion Rates temporarily, they are not considered sustainable because the business will eventually exhaust its customer base and lower its brand to something of a discount outlet store. Worse still, this approach can backfire by triggering a price-cutting spiral, where the prices may have to remain low forever and turn the business into a 'daily deal site' worth buying from only when they are on sale. Not only will this damage the brand's image and set a bad precedent for the future, but it will also lead to Diminishing Rates of Return over time.

In order to build a lasting connection with your leads, make your sales consistent, and ultimately optimize your customer Conversions, having a well-designed Customer Funnel is essential. Otherwise called a marketing or sales funnel, a Customer Funnel refers to the incremental steps that a prospective customer takes on their path to conversion. The more efficient your Customer Funnel is, the higher your Conversion Rate will be.

The idea is that at the top of the funnel, your business casts a wide net to initially capture as many leads as possible. An effective Customer Funnel will incrementally guide and nurture the potential customer through the purchasing decision, with the aim of achieving a purchase at the bottom of the funnel.

Every stage is a micro-conversion that can be optimized to improve lead quality and increase conversions. If a higher-than-average drop-off rate occurs in one of the steps, the data can be analyzed to find potential causes and A/B test improvements. Ultimately, refining your Customer Funnels leads to a more focused and strategic approach that resonates with your audience, and increases your likelihood of a higher Conversion Rate. Better still, a full-funnel marketing strategy picks up after the purchase, and facilitates Customer Retention and audience growth by fostering long-term, high-value relationships.

It can be argued that the most important stages of the Customer Funnel are the ones after the purchase. A sustainable marketing funnel strategy will look to not only increase conversions, but also foster lifelong customers and brand growth.

4.6 CUSTOMER RETENTION & CHURN

If your business is predominantly monetized through subscription sales, then you can skip to *4.6.1 Churn Rate.*

Customer Retention is a business' ability to retain its customers over time. This Metric not only measures the percentage of retained customers by the end of a given time period, but also indicates how successful a business is at satisfying its existing customers.

Before determining your Customer Retention Rate (CRR), there are three numbers you need to measure:

- The amount of customers at the start of a time period (S)
- The amount of customers at the end of that period (E)

- The amount of newly acquired customers during that period (N)

The formula looks like this:

Customer Retention Rate = [(E-N) ÷ S] x 100

For instance, if you had 100 customers at the start of a given month (S) and during that same period you lost five customers and gained 15 new ones (N), then at the end of that month you had 110 customers (E). Using the formula with those numbers your Customer Retention Rate (CRR) for that month would be 95% [(110-15) ÷ 100] x 100]. Ideally, you should be aiming for a 100% retention rate and to not lose a single hard-earned customer. However, a more realistic retention rate for small-to-medium sized online businesses is around 85%. If your CRR is above average, keep up the great work, if your average is significantly lower, it may be worth a closer look at why this is the case.

A high CRR is an excellent indicator of Sustainability and Scalability. In fact, re-engaging existing customers can strengthen and stabilize a brand's revenue growth due to four main factors: Affordability, increased ROI, customer loyalty, and advocacy. Selling to clients you've already built a relationship with is easier and far more cost-effective, because you don't have to use the resources needed for attracting, educating, and converting them from square one. For most businesses, Customer Retention can cost up to seven times less than acquiring a brand new customer. Retention strategies also boost loyalty, resulting in satisfied customers that become advocates of your brand. Their praises and referrals to friends and family bring in more new customers - free of charge - thus driving company growth.

Contrary to common belief, Customer Retention does not start with the Conversion, but rather commences with the very first visit, impression, or any kind of initial contact a prospect has with your business. It relates to how well your Customer Channels create customer loyalty from the very beginning, with a process that nurtures

CHURN RATE BY INDUSTRY

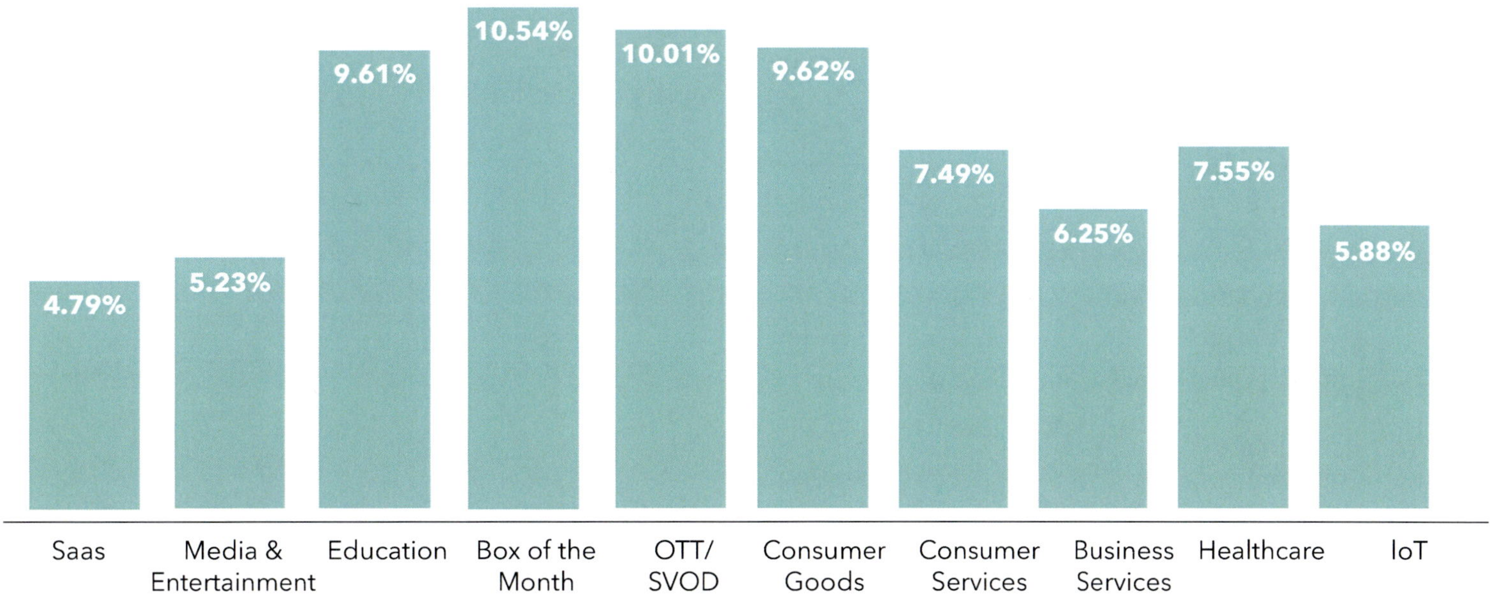

CHURN RATES BY AVERAGE REVENUE PER CUSTOMER (ARPC)

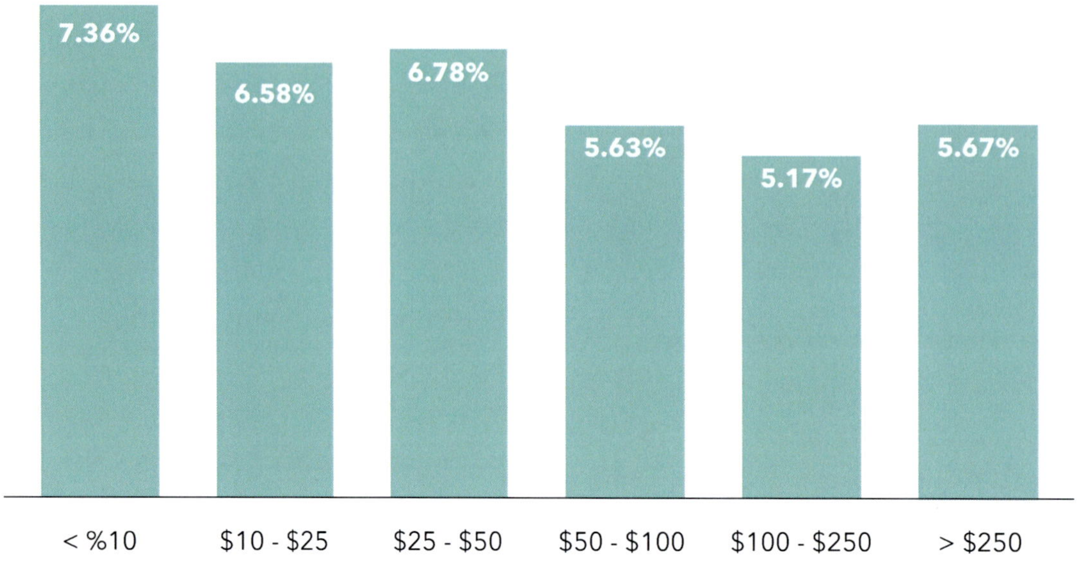

communication, trust, and mutual growth. As your prospects move down the funnel, a customer relationship marketing strategy is key to guiding them beyond the purchase and into advocacy, ultimately leading to an even higher CRR.

Therefore, you should always be looking to improve your customer support, build a consistent consumer experience, and personalize their journey with your company. Creating loyalty programs, offering special discounts/credit to selected customers, crafting engaging emails, and maintaining personal connections on social media are a few ways to make your clients feel valued and appreciated. An updated communication record on your CRM with feedback surveys or any past issues can also be utilized to resolve potential problems and avoid customer churn.

By examining all the factors that lead customers to stick with you, you can better optimize your Customer Retention strategies and prevent them from churning, thus maximizing the Sustainability of your Profits.

4.6.1 CHURN RATE

While your Customer Retention Rate is the percentage of customers who continue to buy from you, your Churn Rate is the percentage of customers who *stop* buying from you. If you own a SaaS business, or any other subscription-based business, then your Churn Rate is the percentage of customers who cancel (or don't renew) their subscription.

A high Churn Rate is an indicator that there is a misalignment between customer expectation and what you're offering. If your customers don't stick around long enough for you to, at least, recuperate the cost of acquiring them in the first place, your business is a long way off from being sustainable.

Naturally, some level of churn is inevitable and occurs for reasons beyond your control, regardless of how much effort you put into keeping your customers happy. So what is an acceptable level of customer churn? Well, that depends on what type of business you own and the market it serves.

For instance, if you own a SaaS business and your average monthly Churn Rate is below 4%, you are kicking ass. If it's between 4% - 7%, you're doing just fine. If it's between 7% - 10%, Buyers won't love it. If it's above 10%, Buyers will start to seriously question the Sustainability and longevity of your SaaS business. However, a 10% monthly Churn Rate for a Subscription eCommerce selling a 'Box of the Month' is considered fairly decent. A study conducted by Recurly Research, benchmarked the average monthly Churn Rate by *industry* in 2021.

Recurly Research also benchmarked the average monthly Churn Rate by price bracket in 2021. As you can see, monthly subscriptions valued under $50 tend to churn at a greater rate than subscriptions at a higher price point.

You don't have to be a mathematician to figure out reducing your Churn Rate is an endeavor worth investing your time in. As mentioned above, the average cost of acquiring a new customer is seven times greater than the cost of maintaining an existing one. For subscription-based businesses, this is even higher, with some SaaS verticals reporting Customer Acquisition Costs of more than 16 times greater than Customer Retention Costs.

No business can afford to lose too many customers, so any forward-thinking company would focus its efforts on low churn, high retention. Preventing churn involves being proactive and constantly looking at ways to improve customer experience. A business that has invested a considerable amount into suppressing its Churn Rate is more likely to produce sustainable results and gain the confidence of prospective Buyers.

4.7 CUSTOMER VALUE

You now know how well your business acquires, converts, and retains its customers. But what is the *true value* of your average customer? This is the question that's on the tip of everyone's tongue.

According to Hubspot, the average cost of acquiring customers online has increased by 50% between 2015 and 2020. This increased competition means that businesses have to constantly improve their Customer Channels to achieve a positive return on their efforts.

Let's quickly reflect on four important Metrics touched on in Chapter 3.6 that we can use to determine Customer Value:

- Customer Acquisition Cost (CAC)
- Lifetime Value (LTV)
- Customer Lifetime Value (CLV)
- LTV:CAC Ratio

Frustratingly, the internet offers a variety of ways to calculate these Metrics, and often confuses the true meaning of Customer Lifetime Value (CLV), which is the average gross revenue a customer represents to your business (LTV), minus the cost of acquiring that customer in the first place (CAC).

Comparing LTV with CAC can help evaluate the viability of your acquisition, Conversion and retention strategy. Put simply, if the CAC exceeds the expected LTV, then the acquisition model is unsustainable and will eventually lead to losses.

Customer Lifetime Value = LTV - CAC

If LTV = \$19 and CAC = \$20, then your CLV is -\$1 (\$19 - \$20 = -\$1)

And if you're only breaking even, then what's the point?

If LTV = \$20 and CAC = \$20, then your CLV is \$0 (\$20 - \$20 = \$0)

Another important Customer Value Metric you need to be aware of is your CAC:LTV ratio. Although it varies depending on your Business Model and market, a healthy ratio is generally considered to be 3:1 or higher. This means that for every dollar spent on acquiring a customer (CAC), the customer spends three dollars (LTV) with your business.

If LTV = \$60 and CAC = \$20, then your LTV:CAC Ratio = 3:1 (60 ÷20 = 3)

So, what is the *true* Customer Lifetime Value (CLV)?

If LTV = \$60 and CAC = \$20, then your CLV is \$40 (\$60 - \$20 = \$40)

Studies over the past 20 years have shown that most businesses fail within their first five years of operations. Many of them generate plenty of sales and revenue, but without getting the customer acquisition math right, the cost eventually brings them to their knees. So, why don't more owners focus on this Metric?

Probably because CAC is not only difficult to measure, but it also brings the unpleasant realization that your hard-earned customers are not always valuable. In fact, if most of your customers are too expensive to retain, they can do your business more harm than good. Failing to track, measure and compare Customer Value is like flying a plane blind. Naturally, it becomes obvious why potential buyers will pay close attention to Customer Value Metrics to establish the Sustainability of your business.

In closing, Sustainability is a significant driver of value because it largely determines the likelihood of your business sustaining or improving its performance and therefore the risk profile presented to potential acquirers.

By now, you should know how sustainable your business is and what you can do to bolster this over time. Always be looking to strengthen your product/service offering to improve retention and therefore Customer Value. Look at ways to strengthen your resilience to the always-changing market conditions. Diversify your Customer Channels if your business is heavily dependent on a single source. Optimize your Customer Acquisition Channels to boost conversions, and invest in Retention strategies to achieve sustainable and scalable growth.

If you keep these principles in mind whilst developing and operating your business, I'd be willing to bet that the value of your business will increase exponentially.

ACTIVITY 4A

Gauging Sustainability

1. Determine whether each sustainability aspect of your business creates Upward, Downward or Neutral pressure on the Multiplier
2. Score the likely impact this pressure will have on your Multiplier out of 3 (1 or -1 = small impact, 2 or -2 = big impact, 3 or -3 = huge impact)
3. Calculate the total pressure applied to your Multiplier
   a. Sum of Upward Pressure impact points (e.g. 5)
   b. Sum of Downward Pressure impact points (e.g -3)
   c. Subtract Downward Pressure impact points from Upward Pressure impact points (5-3 = 2)
   d. If you're feeling unsure about how a particular aspect of your performance will impact your Multiplier, refer to the content above, talk to a friend, or an advisor, and of course there's always Google.

If you're feeling unsure about how a particular aspect of your performance will impact your Multiplier, refer to the content above, talk to a friend, or an advisor, and of course there's always Google.

METRIC	PRESSURE	IMPACT
E.g. Quality of Product / Service Offering	*↓ Downward Pressure*	*- 3*
Market Resilience		
Channel Diversity		
Customer Retention Rate (and/or Churn Rate)		
Customer Value		
	TOTAL PRESSURE =	

If your pressure total number is positive, your performance will create Upward Pressure on the Multiplier and if it's negative, it will create Downward Pressure on the Multiplier. If the pressure total is between 5 and -5, a small amount of pressure will be applied to the Multiplier. If the pressure total is between 10 and -10, a greater amount of pressure will be applied, and so on. While we can't calculate an exact figure to add or subtract to your Base Multiplier, you should have a sense of whether your Multiplier is higher, lower or the same after completing this activity.

ACTIVITY 4B

Action Items

Brainstorm any aspects of your business that could be worked on to improve its sustainability and overall value. Describe how it would improve sustainability, what resources it would require, and the likely impact it would have on your Multiplier by taking this action. Even if you're feeling unsure about some of your ideas, write them down anyway. Remember, this is just an exercise.

ACTION	HOW	RESOURCES	IMPACT
E.g. Improve Channel Diversity	*Invest in email marketing and content / SEO to reduce dependency on Facebook ads.*	*Create a weekly newsletter and hire a content writer.*	*Medium*

KEY TAKEAWAYS

SUSTAINABILITY GAUGE

- Key factors that determine how sustainable your business is:
    - Product and Service Offering
    - Market Resilience
    - Customer Channels
    - Channel Diversity
    - Customer Conversion
    - Customer Retention & Churn
    - Customer Value

- **Product/Service Offering:** The quality of your product and service offering forms the foundation of your entire business and has a major influence on its ability to sustain performance over time. Strengthening your offering will improve Customer Retention and value.

- **Market Resilience:** Your business' ability to sustain performance during economic downturns, market disruptions, and other adversities.
    - Some Business Models and industries are inherently more resilient than others.
    - It is important to distinguish whether your business is Viral or Trending businesses vs Evergreen.
    - It's also important to distinguish between Trends and Emerging Markets.

- **Customer Channels:** The sales, marketing and business development activities that you use to attract potential leads and convert them into paying customers. Buyers will evaluate how sustainable each channel is based on your Channel Diversity, acquisition, conversion, and retention strategies.

- **Channel Diversity:** Buyers will investigate your Website Traffic Sources, Third Party Platform analytics and statistics, as well as your Direct/Offline Customer Channels to assess the diversity and therefore Sustainability of your customer acquisition strategies. A heavily on a single Customer Channel is usually considered a lot riskier than a business acquiring customers through multiple channels.

- **Customer Conversion:** Is the way in which you convert customers sustainable? Businesses that are constantly running flash sales and large discounts eventually exhaust their audience and experience Diminishing Rates of Return over time. A well-designed Customer Funnel will optimize your Customer Conversion and help you achieve consistent sales.

- **Customer Retention and Churn:** High-retention, low-churn businesses often yield high Valuations because they are generally more scalable and more profitable. This is because the cost of retaining a customer is significantly less than acquiring a new customer and the Customer Lifetime Value is significantly higher.

- **Customer Value:** Some customers can be lucrative, while others can render you bankrupt. Brokers, Valuers, and the more savvy buyers will calculate the *true value* of your customers, by properly measuring your Customer Acquisition Cost (CAC), Lifetime Value (LTV), true Customer Lifetime Value (CLV), and your LTV:CAC Ratio.

GAUGING DEFENSIBILITY

5

5. GAUGING DEFENSIBILITY

To explain the concept of Defensibility, let me paint a picture. Imagine a lemonade stand (yes, very original I know) in a leafy suburb at the beginning of summer. Nobody else in the neighborhood is selling lemonade except for a young entrepreneur named Jenny, aged 9. Business is *booming*. Out of nowhere, her next-door neighbor Taylor (also 9) has a grapefruit tree in her backyard and decides to set up a stall of her own. *How defensible is Jenny's business to this potential new entrant?* What would it take for Taylor to set up shop and compete for customers? The grapefruits from her tree, a trestle table, and a cardboard sign - *that's it*. From what we know about Jenny's business so far, we would consider it to be relatively *indefensible*, right?

But what if I now tell you that by midsummer, there was a lemonade stand on every corner in the neighborhood and Jenny's was still by far the most popular... You might be wondering why or how Jenny has been able to defend her market share with more than 10 new entrants all vying for the same customers in her neighborhood?

"Was it because she was first to market?"

"Is it because her lemonade is the tastiest?"

"Or the most affordable?"

"Does she have the best customer service?"

"Does she have clever branding?"

"Could it be the special fertilizer her dad uses to nourish the lemon tree in her backyard?"

The truth is, you'll never know because Jenny forgot to install Google Analytics, so there's no way of tracking customer behavior, ha! We'll revisit Jenny's lemonade stand later on, but for now, let's re-focus our attention on your business.

For your business, Defensibility is measured by its ability to defend market share. I've seen businesses on both ends of the spectrum and everything in between. On one end, you have businesses that can be replicated in a matter of weeks at little cost, and on the other end, you have businesses that would take competitors and new entrants many years and millions of dollars to develop a competitive market-ready alternative.

In this day and age, where web hosting can cost as little as a buck a month, the former is far more common than the latter. As I'm sure you already know, the more defensible your business is, the lower the perceived risk of losing market share, and generally speaking, the more buyers will pay for your business.

Defensibility Pressures create more Upward Pressure than Downward Pressure on the Multiplier

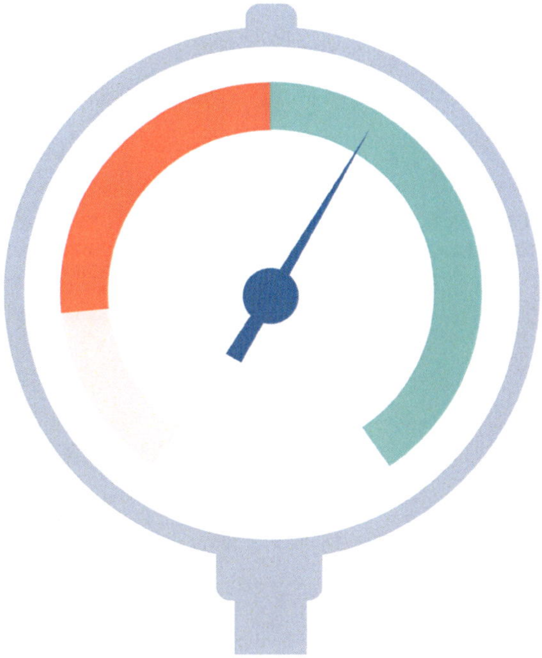

Your business would have to score quite low in Defensibility for it to have any major negative impact on your Multiplier, however should your business score above average you can expect a decent boost to your valuation.

But how exactly do you measure Defensibility? How do you know if your business is at high risk of being replicated or eclipsed by competitors and new entrants? In this Chapter, we will look at the eight common Defense Barriers that will gain you big bonus points from valuers and prospective Buyers. But before we do, let's have a bit of fun and take a look at a business that scores a big fat 0 when it comes to Defensibility.

5.1 NO DEFENSE BARRIER WHATSOEVER

It has never been easier to create a profitable online store in less than a month by setting up a Shopify store, sourcing generic products on Alibaba, and funneling Traffic to the site through highly targeted Facebook ads. These businesses – let's call them 'Facebook Dropshippers' – can generate significant Profits in a very short amount of time. However, there is almost nothing stopping a new entrant from sourcing the same products and bidding on the same advertising keywords. These businesses usually have a very short shelf life unless the owners are keeping abreast of viral Trends and responding quickly by updating their product mix with the new flavor of the day.

Model	Dropship eCommerce
Age	4 months
Earnings	$40,000 / month
Traffic Source	99% Facebook ads
Supplier	Various manufacturers found on Alibaba

Facebook Dropshippers typically rank amongst the lowest in Defensibility, popularity and - surprise, surprise - their Earnings Multiplier Score. Despite being easily replicable and completely indefensible, demand for these businesses does exist, albeit at a much lower Multiplier. Now that you know what a completely indefensible business looks like, it's high time we explored how businesses develop effective Defense Barriers and how you might go about erecting one or two of your own.

5.2 DEFENSE BARRIERS

Defense Barriers or *Barriers to Entry* can manifest

within a business in many ways. However, there are eight common barriers we see most often. In no particular order, these are:

1. Network Economies
2. Switching Costs
3. Brand Loyalty
4. Intellectual Property
5. Lowest Price
6. Economies of Scale
7. Organic Search
8. Start-up Costs

As we explore each barrier, you will notice that some barriers are stronger than others; some are inherent to a particular Business Model, and some barriers can be systematically cultivated through clever strategic planning and meticulous execution.

5.2.1 NETWORK ECONOMIES

Network Economies is where a business develops a Defensive Barrier through a concept called the *Network Effect*, which we touched on briefly in 2.1.5. The Network Effect comes into play when the increased number of Users exponentially improves the quality of a product or service offering.

There is no better industry to exemplify this phenomenon than with GPS Navigation Applications. If your application is being used by 100 people every month, it is fair to say that the navigational information generated would be extremely limited, making it difficult to attract new Users with a relatively weak offering. Now let's consider a market leader like Waze.com, who as of the beginning of 2022, have more than 140 million monthly Users. Each new Waze User improves the accuracy of their data and therefore the quality of their product, making it progressively easier to acquire the next User.

Simply put, more Users leads to even more Users, which leads to higher and higher Defense Barriers, which leads to a higher and higher Valuation. I can't say for sure what Multiplier Waze was acquired for, but I can tell you that Google paid a fair bit ($1.3 billion).

Online forums like Quora.com and Marketplaces like Airbnb.com have some of the highest Defense Barriers thanks to their Network Economies. Each company first had to reach a critical mass of Users before they were able to attract mainstream appeal. This is usually an organic process, and once a business reaches a tipping point, it's incredibly challenging for new entrants to gain a foothold, because customers want to use the platform everyone else is currently using. This is why forum and Marketplace businesses are amongst some of the strongest market defenders.

Let's compare two businesses that are monetized through the generation of fishing content.

	Fishing Blog	Fishing Forum
Model	Affiliate blog	Advertising forum
Description	A fishing blog that reviews the latest fishing equipment and generates revenue through affiliate commissions.	The go-to forum for all things fishing with 10 million monthly Users sharing their favorite fishing tips, locations and stories.
Network Economy	No	Yes
Founded	2010	2010
Earnings	$1 million	$1.5 million
Multiplier	3x	5x
Valuation	$3 million	$5 million

All things equal, the fishing forum is likely to sell for a much higher Earnings Multiplier than a fishing blog, because it benefits from Network Economies and therefore has a significantly stronger Defense Barrier.

5.2.2 SWITCHING COSTS

The term Switching Costs refers to the time, resources, money, and mental effort a customer pays when they switch to an alternative brand. The higher the cost of switching, the less likely a customer is to replace your brand with an alternative, and therefore, the stronger your defense barrier will be.

Many successful companies build high Switching Costs into their product and service offering in order to lock customers into their ecosystems and discourage them from switching to a competitor. Here are some common examples of Switching Costs:

- **Termination Fee:** Many mobile phone companies require a two-year contract and charge high fees for canceling prematurely.
- **Lengthy Cancellation Process:** Service providers usually incorporate a complex and Lengthy Cancellation Process with significant waiting time and paperwork involved.
- **Technological Incompatibility:** Software and hardware companies apply the lock-in platform trap, like the Apple Watch, which supports iPhones and iPads exclusively.
- **Consumable Trap:** Many companies lock their customers by being the exclusive provider of the consumables for their base product, like Hewlett-Packard with the cartridges for their printers.
- **Data Migration:** Migrating company data is always challenging when switching to a different cloud storage provider, and it often involves transferring large capacities of terabytes or even petabytes. Additional issues of limited bandwidth and possible download fees reinforce the potential loss of data.
- **Data Trap:** The supreme product personalization that brands like Spotify offer is not just for additional Customer Value, but also to encourage (or force, really) customers to think twice before losing all that customized data upon exit.
- **Industry Standard Trap:** Several companies have positioned their products as the 'industry

standard' accepted by the vast majority of the public, just like the Microsoft Office format is most commonly accepted as opposed to the free OpenOffice alternative.

- **Learning Curve Trap:** The time and expense of learning, configuring, and customizing a new product/device/software creates a significant learning curve. Companies like Adobe and Salesforce offer a great value proposition, accessible only to those who become proficient in using their software. With many of them becoming certified experts, switching to a different solution would not only mean going through the learning process again, but also wasting that acquired skill.

Regardless of whether you marvel in its genius or scoff at its wickedness, Switching Costs can prove to be a highly effective Defense Barrier for your business. That said, consumers are starting to wise up and consider the future switching cost and the ethics of the company they buy from into their initial purchasing decision. Let's compare two well-known businesses that exemplify high and low switching costs:

	WPEngine.com	vs	Spotify.com
Model	SaaS		SaaS
Description	Sells website hosting subscriptions		Sells music media subscriptions
Switching Cost	Low		High
Reason	All data is transferable		Loss of all customized content

By reasonable assumption and all other things being equal; Spotify is more Defensible than WPEngine because of its higher Switching Costs. Spotify offers a vast catalog of songs and artists, and curates personalized music playlists that match a User's taste. The software notifies you when your favorite artists release a new song or play a concert near you. It even creates a playlist and introduces you to new music based on the type of music you have been listening to recently.

The catch is that these perks can be enjoyed exclusively on Spotify's subscription platform and all that customized content cannot be migrated to a different application, which is what I explained above as a Data Trap. Leaving the Spotify platform for another streaming service would mean letting go of all your saved playlists to rebuild them on a new interface, and giving up Spotify's features of improving your daily listening experience. Most people would think twice before losing all that, which is how Spotify has such a high retention and low Churn Rate.

5.2.3 BRAND LOYALTY

Brand Loyalty can act as a strong defense barrier because it cannot be re-created overnight. Rather, it is cultivated by providing a consistent customer experience over a sustained period of time. For instance, when was the last time you used a search engine that wasn't Google? I'll bet that for most of you readers, it was a long time ago. That's because Google's search engine is the most powerful, reliable and user-friendly. It is because of Google's strong brand and excellent customer service that the multinational has been able to consistently enter and dominate new markets at breakneck speeds.

Strong Brand Loyalty is demonstrated when customers trust the products and services of a certain business so much that they ignore alternatives that may be more affordable or better suited to their needs. They become not only loyal consumers, but also advocates of the brand by promoting it to their family and friends. A devoted customer base affects the business' revenue, growth, reputation and value on the market.

Let's compare the two online stores below:

	Tessa's Online Store	vs	Jackie's Online Store
Customer Review Rating	3.5 stars		5 stars
Repeat Customer Rate	17%		48%
Churn Rate	17%		5%
Brand Loyalty	Poor		Strong
Defense Barrier	Low		High

5.2.4 INTELLECTUAL PROPERTY

Intellectual Property (IP) such as contracts, patents, and licenses can make it difficult for new entrants when an existing business owns the license or patent in question. When companies develop a new idea or prototype, they often apply for a patent, thus putting legal restrictions and creating a high Barrier for new entrants. If a competing tech startup wants to enter the very same market, it has two options: either wait for this legal protection to expire – running the risk of losing market momentum – or use a different formula to produce a substitute product/service, which in most cases includes a lot of investment and some possible legal risks.

Let's take a look at two businesses that both sell physical products:

	Anaconda	vs	Amazon
Model	eCommerce		Transactional / Marketplace
Description	Sells outdoor camping and sporting clothing and equipment.		Facilitates the purchase and sale of many, many different products.
Founded	2004		1994
Intellectual Property	No		Yes
Defense Barrier	Moderate		High

The USPTO granted Amazon the '1-Click' patent in 1999, which gave them the exclusive rights to single-click buying for the better part of two decades. During this time, Amazon's impenetrable Defense Barrier gave them an insurmountable advantage over other online retailers. Although businesses like Anaconda have now been able to utilize '1-Click' buying since 2017, they have little chance of competing with Amazon now, who has since developed several other Defense Barriers (Lowest Price, Search Rankings, Advertising Spend, Economies of Scale, etc.).

5.2.5 LOWEST PRICE

Offering the Lowest Prices is an old-school

technique typically used by larger companies to kill off competition by offering products and services at prices where competitors and new entrants struggle to make a Profit. Some companies use predatory pricing to gain market share when penetrating new markets, or with the hope that the lured shoppers will buy additional products and become loyal to the brand. The company that sets this strategy is often losing money too, but is usually backed by Investors with deep pockets, allowing the company to sustain losses for as long as it takes to drive out its competitors.

There is no better example of this than Uber, which, up until November 2021, had never turned over a single dollar in profit since it was founded in 2009. Despite reporting 11 straight years of losses, the company has mercilessly outperformed taxi services with their unbeatable prices.

	Taxis	vs	Uber
Airport Fair	$49		$37

A Lower Price Barrier is usually a stepping stone towards a more organic and sustainable Barrier such as Economies of Scale, Network Economies or Brand Loyalty. As such, business analysts believe that Uber will increase their prices once they are confident they have developed other Defense Barriers around their business.

This Defense barrier is usually reserved for businesses with deep pockets from significant private investment. Unfortunately for most small business owners, engaging in a Lowest Price strategy isn't a tactic I can recommend. Before you try it out, you need to be aware of the potential risks and pitfalls. For instance, your brand may become affiliated with "cheap" or "low quality" products and services. You might upset customers, who feel ripped off for buying your products at your pre-discounted rate. Last but not least, your competitors may respond by lowering *their* prices, which leaves you with two no-good options; conceding defeat and losing your pricing advantage or engaging in a pricing war, which can be a dangerous race to the bottom.

5.2.6 ECONOMIES OF SCALE

Depending on the market in which your business operates, Economies of Scale may be a Defense Barrier that is out of reach. That's because Economies of Scale is only achieved when you have a *Cost Advantage* or a *Spending Advantage* over your competitors - since Economies of Scale are cost advantages enjoyed by brands when production becomes efficient.

To have a Cost Advantage, you must be able to mass produce or *bulk buy* in quantities that achieve a lower price per unit than your competitors. To have a Spending Advantage, you must be able to spend more money on advertising and promotion than your competitors. In other words, you not only have to be big - you need to be bigger than everybody else.

Cost Advantage: As you can see in the table on the following page, Kate is dominating the online Candles & Essential Oils market and Ted is struggling to compete on price because Kate is able to bulk buy at a discounted rate.

Spending Advantage: If Kate doesn't want to compete on price, she could increase her price to $150 and re-invest the extra $30 she makes per unit sold into advertising and promotion. Unfortunately for Ted, his tiny marketing budget isn't big enough to gain his store any visibility on the first page of Google for any of the popular keywords and search terms.

	Ted's Store	Kate's Store
Model	eCommerce	eCommerce
Niche	Candles & Essential Oils	Candles & Essential Oils
Founded	2020	2009
Monthly Sales	$12,000	$700,000
Supplier Discount	0%	20%
Wholesale Price	$100	$80
Retail Price	$150	$120
Economies of Scale	No	Yes

Meanwhile, as Kate's Store continues to grow, the greater her Economies of Scale, and therefore Defensibility, becomes.

	Ted's Store	Kate's Store
Marketing Budget	$500 / month	$50,000 / month
Economies of Scale	No	Yes

5.2.7 ORGANIC SEARCH

Nowadays, a customer's journey usually begins on Google's search page. Therefore, visibility on search engines is critical, and Search Rankings can represent a robust Barrier to Entry. Today's competition might be one-click away, but your business' positioning in Search Rankings will define just how far away that click is...Put simply, the easier your site is to find, the more customers you will get, as shoppers rarely get past the first page of Google's search results.

Some of you readers will have built a strong Defense Barrier around your business by investing significant time, energy, and resources into Content Marketing and Search Engine Optimization (SEO). Unlike other Defense Barriers, you don't necessarily need to be the biggest to win. You can be the small fry (the underdog!) and appear on the first page for relevant search terms. Unless Google's algorithm changes, competitors and new entrants cannot take your keyword positions overnight. They will have to roll up their sleeves and produce high-quality content just like you have. Having said that, larger competitors do have the firepower to hire dedicated content and SEO teams to climb the rankings a lot faster than you or I could hope to.

	All Things Tennis	Tennis 24/7
Model	eCommerce	eCommerce
Description	Sells tennis equipment	Sells tennis equipment
Top 3 SERPs*	25, 33, 44	1, 1, 2
Visibility	Low	High
Barrier	Low	High

**SERPs stands for Search Engine Ranking Positions*

Generally speaking, the higher your Organic Search Rankings, the more Defensible your business will be. Hence why 'Tennis 24/7' is considered more Defensible and therefore more valuable than 'All Things Tennis'.

5.2.8 STARTUP COSTS

Startup Costs can act as a Defense Barrier when a company develops a product or service that requires significant capital investment to get started. There are always some Startup Costs involved when entering a market, and depending on the industry; they can be minimal or substantial – including, but not limited to, infrastructure, equipment, permits, licenses, etc.

This is by far the weakest Barrier in today's market, because there are so many open-source solutions, third-party services, and licenses available, that a new entrant can often test the market before making any significant investment in platform technology. However, combined with other Barriers, high Startup Costs can reinforce other obstacles and weaken a potential firm's ability to enter the industry.

Defending Market Share in Highly Competitive Markets

A highly competitive market poses equally as much risk of failure as it does the opportunity for growth. It all depends on your business' ability to *defend and win* market share. As I've explained, there are many Barriers you can build around your business to improve its Defensibility and market value - some are stronger than others.

However, even the strongest Defense Barrier won't be enough to defend market share from the big guys like Google, Facebook and Quora. We've seen Google Search render thousands of information aggregator websites redundant in the blink of an eye. We've seen Facebook Ads dominate the digital advertising space, leaving barely a morsel for the boutique ad networks. We've also seen Quora become *the* online forum, making it more and more difficult for smaller niche forums to survive.

So pick your fight. Know when to defend your turf and when to pivot. While Barriers are undoubtedly valuable and far from futile, you can argue that the greatest Defense a business can have is its ability to adapt and pivot when new threats or opportunities arise. This dynamism has a lot more to do with the Leadership and Culture (9.13) within your business, rather than the business itself. We'll go into this in more depth in the next Chapter when we look at how Scalability drives value.

ACTIVITY 5A

So, how Defensible is Your Business?

1. List any defense barriers you think your business has.

2. Rate the defensibility of your business on a scale between 0 and 5; 0 being a Facebook Dropshipper (5.1), 1 being the average small business in a competitive market with no mentionable defense barriers, and 5 being a business with almost impenetrable defense barriers.

Keep in mind that the overwhelming majority of small, owner-operated businesses don't have any significant defense barriers simply by virtue of being small. If you fit this description, there's no need to be discouraged, because unless you're a Facebook Dropshipper it's very unlikely to result in any Downward Pressure on your Multiplier.

ACTIVITY 5B

Improving defensibility

List any defense barriers you believe you could realistically develop or strengthen. Describe how it would improve defensibility, what resources it would require, and the likely impact it would have on your Multiplier by taking this action. Even if you're feeling unsure about some of your ideas, write them down anyway. Remember, this is just an exercise.

ACTION	HOW	RESOURCES	IMPACT
E.g. Organic Search	*Invest in content marketing and search engine optimization*	*SEO strategist and content writer(s)*	*Medium*

KEY TAKEAWAYS

DEFENSIBILITY GAUGE

- Defensibility is measured by a business's ability to defend its market share. Highly Defensible businesses are ones that cannot be easily replicated or eclipsed by existing competitors and new entrants.

- The more Defensible your business is, the less risk there is of losing market share, and therefore the more valuable your business will be in the eyes of brokers, valuers and most importantly, potential acquirers.

- Some Defense Barriers are easier to cultivate than others. Some Defense Barriers are stronger than others. The eight primary Barriers explored in this Chapter are; Network Economies, Switching Costs, Brand Loyalty, Intellectual property, Lowest Price, Economies of Scale, Organic Search, and Startup Costs.

- **Network Economies** is achieved when you reach a tipping point where each new customer you acquire improves the experience for all of your customers. This Barrier is usually exclusive to transactional or user-generated Business Models.

- **Switching Costs** refers to the time, resources, money and mental effort required from a customer to switch your product or service out for an alternative. Common techniques include Termination Fees, incompatible devices, Data Traps, difficult migration, and learning curve.

- **Brand Loyalty** is when customers trust your products and services so much that they ignore alternatives that may be more affordable or better suited to their needs. A strong brand is unique and not easily replicable, serving as a strong Defense Barrier for many businesses.

- **Intellectual Property** can make it difficult for new and existing firms to compete when you own the exclusive distribution rights for a particular product or service.

- **Lowest Price** is an old-school technique used by larger companies to kill off competition by offering products and services at prices where competitors and new entrants struggle to make a Profit. Although considered outdated by man, 21st-Century companies like Uber still experience significant success with this strategy.

- **Economies of Scale** is largely reserved for big businesses who can leverage their 'Cost Advantage' to outprice smaller competitors and exploit their 'Spending Advantage' to dominate Paid Search, Display Advertising and Social Media.

- **Organic Search** has proved to be an invaluable Defense Barrier for small online businesses because, unlike other Defense Barriers, you don't need to be big to win.

- **Startup Costs:** This is by far the weakest Barrier in today's market, because there are so many open-source and third-party solutions that a new entrant can test the market with before making any significant investment in platform technology.

- Whilst it is worth investing time in developing Defense Barriers around your business, the greatest Defense a business can have is its ability to adapt and pivot when new threats or opportunities arise.

GAUGING SCALABILITY

6

6. GAUGING SCALABILITY

The term *scalable* is one of the most overused buzzwords in business, which explains why there are so many different interpretations of its meaning. For the purposes of valuing an online business, I want to set some boundaries around its meaning and define Scalability as the ability by which a company can grow its Revenue while maintaining or reducing its cost base.

Growth vs. Scalability

It is essential to distinguish the difference between *growth* and *Scalability*. A business with high growth potential is not necessarily scalable. For instance, if a business doubles its Revenue, but at the same time doubles its operating costs, the business has *grown*, but it has not *scaled*. The comparison table below demonstrates the difference between growing a business and scaling a business.

See what I mean? Although Business A has achieved significant growth, it has not demonstrated an ability to scale effectively. This is because the margin between Revenue and Expenses has stayed more or less the same. Whereas Business B has demonstrated an ability to scale because its Profit margin increases exponentially as sales increase.

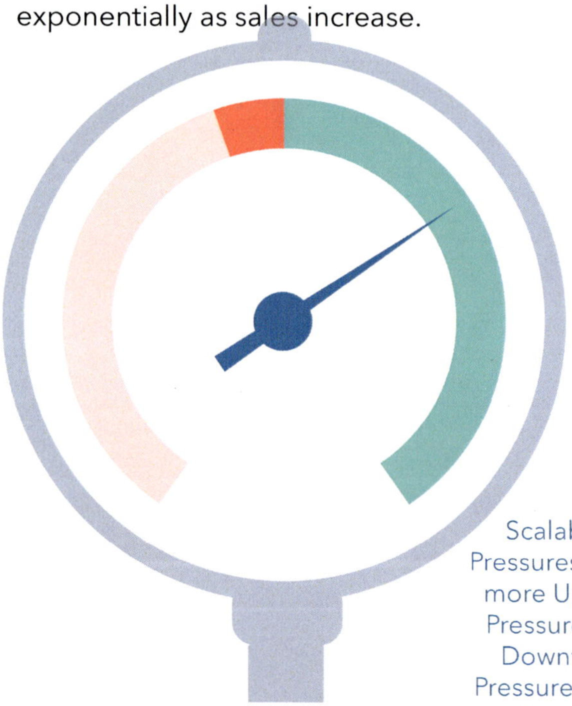

Scalability Pressures create more Upward Pressure than Downward Pressure on the Multiplier

A GROWING BUSINESS VS A SCALING BUSINESS

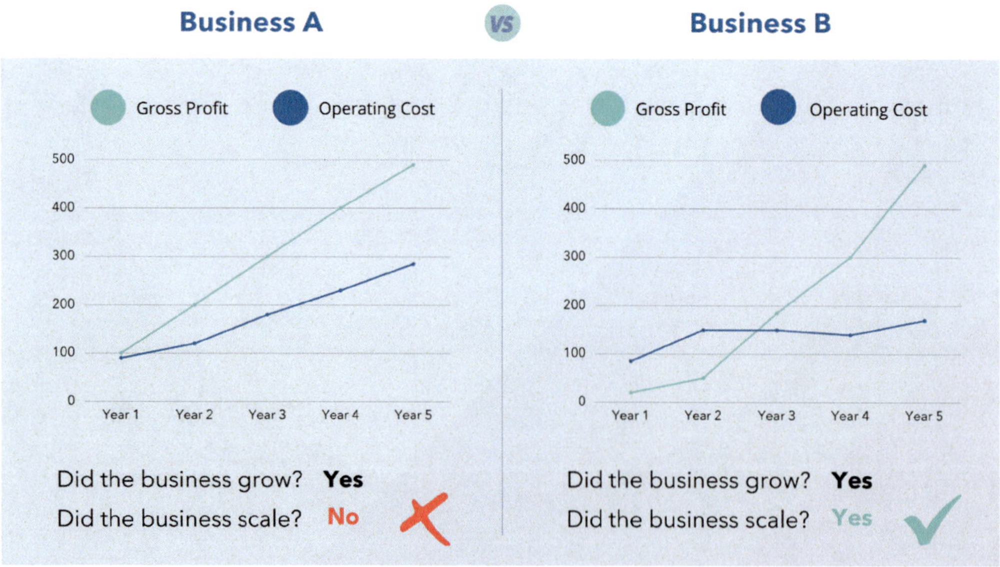

The Scalability Gauge is more likely to detect Upward Pressures than Downward Pressures because many of the negative scalability pressures are captured in Base Multiplier, Performance and Sustainability Gauges. As we have learned some business models are inherently more scalable

than others, which is why a SaaS business begins with a higher Base Multiplier than a Services business.

6.1 HOW SCALABLE IS YOUR BUSINESS MODEL?

As you can see, some Business Models are inherently more scalable than others. If you don't already know, Dealflow (far left) is a digital services company I ran for many years providing M&A advisory services. So why does Dealflow have a lower scalability score than the average digital services business?

Well, under my leadership, Dealflow provided a one-to-one, end-to-end, tailored service offering. As our client base grew, so too did our team of advisors. As you know, human resources are often a business' heaviest operating cost and this is especially true with a service that requires specialist knowledge in Mergers and Acquisitions; Finance, Contract Law, Business Development, Digital Marketing and Valuations. Furthermore, Dealflow operated on a negative Cash Flow Cycle, which means we only invoiced our clients once we had completed the service in full. Even then, we only invoiced clients if the acquisition was successful.

There are, of course, exceptions to this rule, where digital services businesses have been able to heavily standardize and productize their offering to significantly improve the Scalability of their business. While we see these businesses sell for higher Multipliers than a fully tailored one-to-one service like Dealflow could ever hope for, they still typically sell for significantly less than other Business Models like SaaS and Transactional business models.

Physical Product eCommerce businesses (including FBA and Dropship models) are generally considered to be the second-lowest ranking Business Model from a Scalability perspective because the Cost of Goods Sold (CoGS) are baked into every customer purchase. As the customer base grows, so does the CoGS. The only exception to this rule is if your business grows to

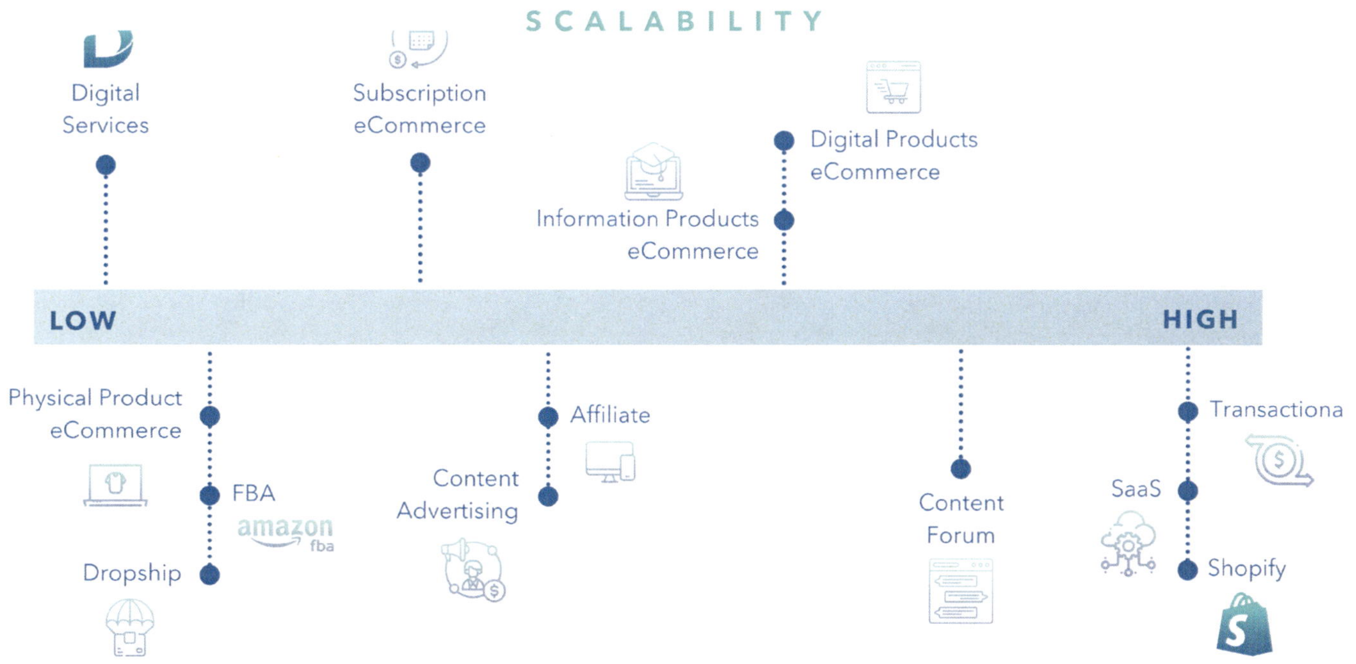

a size where it benefits from Economies of Scale (5.2.6), where stronger buying power and better margins allow a business to scale to some degree, albeit not nearly to the same degree as SaaS and Transactional Business Models. Subscription eCommerce businesses cannot avoid CoGS either, but the positive Cash Flow cycle and predictability of recurring revenue does provide a distinct advantage when it comes to growing a business and is often interpreted as being slightly more scalable than other physical product eCommerce models.

Digital Products and Information Products eCommerce, as well as Advertising and Affiliate content Business Models are generally considered more scalable, due to their ability to grow sales with relatively low marginal increases in operational cost. That is to say, the cost of producing the digital product or content doesn't necessarily increase when more customers purchase the product or visit the website to read its content. Forums and online communities rank slightly higher again because the content is user-generated and can scale exponentially once reaching critical mass and igniting the Network Effect (5.2.1).

So why is Shopify one of the most scalable businesses on the planet? For starters, SaaS and Transactional businesses are typically considered the most scalable Business Models, because the cost-per-customer typically reduces exponentially as the business grows. Once the product or platform has been built, it is possible to scale up at a relatively low cost, provided there is a healthy ratio between Customer Acquisition Cost (CAC) and Lifetime Value (LTV). Shopify's Business Model is both SaaS and Transactional, whereby Revenue is generated through (a) recurring subscriptions fees, (b) commission fees every time a vendor sells a product, and (c) commission fees when a vendor decides to sell their business on Shopify Exchange. Put simply, each new vendor that signs up Shopify typically represents thousands, if not tens of thousands, of dollars in Revenue and presumably very minimal additional operating cost to their business.

Whilst the above graphic helps you understand the inherent Scalability of different Business Models along a spectrum, it is by no means an exact science or a comprehensive measure. Over the past decade I have seen Digital Product eCommerce businesses that are more scalable than some SaaS businesses, due to other determinants related to product/service offering, operating procedure and market positioning.

6.2 HOW SCALABLE ARE YOUR OPERATIONS?

Buyers will assess the way your business operates to determine how well the current team, systems and processes are likely to respond to rapid growth. An ambitious buyer might be hoping to increase sales revenue by 3x in the first year of the acquisition, and therefore needs to determine whether the business can handle that many customers, and at what cost.

Nothing exposes weak points in your systems and processes better than significant growth over a short period of time. Whether you have experienced this in your own business or not, I'm sure you will agree that a certain modus operandi is better equipped to handle the onslaught of a burgeoning customer demand far better than others. It really comes down to how well the systems and processes have been integrated,

	Business A	Business B
Model	FBA	FBA
Revenue	$880,000	$880,000
Date Founded	2016	2016
Time Commitment	~30 hours/wk	~10 hours/wk
Multiplier	2.9x	3.2x
Automation & Optimization	Uses Hubspot CRM software to track the sales pipeline, and Mailchimp to send out monthly newsletters.	Fully integrated Technology Stack; all Customer Funnels integrate with the website, Hubspot, Mailchimp, Asana, and other Third-Party Platforms. Customer data is auto-synced across all platforms and operational systems and processes have been optimized for maximum efficiency.
Documentation	No documentation because the owner and team know what to do.	Standard Operating Procedure (SOP) document detailing all systems, processes, resources and training guides.
Team	1 Owner-operator 1 Full-time staff 2 Part-time contractors	1 Passive owner 1 Full-time manager 1 Full-time staff 1 Part-time staff

optimized, automated and documented. Last but not least, the team who carries out these operational tasks and/or oversees them, will also have a considerable influence on a business' ability to scale. Let's compare two businesses that I brokered in 2018 to better explain what I mean.

Now pretend you were looking to buy one of these businesses. Which one would be easier to scale? The obvious answer is Business B, but why? Business A had barely optimized or automated their business, which meant that when sales increased, the owner's time would increase significantly as well. Although Business A used Hubspot's CRM to track its sales pipeline, it was not integrated with the website, Mailchimp, or any of its other Third-Party Platforms.

This meant that whenever someone interacted with the website, be it subscribing to the newsletter, filling out a contact form, or making a purchase, the owner of Business A had to manually record these interactions in their Hubspot CRM, or the valuable data was lost to the ether.

Let's give Business A the benefit of the doubt

and assume that they *did* manually record these interactions into Hubspot (they didn't, by the way). If you acquired Business A and scaled it to 5x its original size, you would need to hire more staff to keep up with the manual data entry and other administrative tasks - not to mention the time-cost of training staff with no documented procedures.

In contrast, Business B is well prepared for rapid growth, because all systems and processes have been integrated, optimized and automated. When customer demand surges, each customer receives the exact same experience through well-optimized funnels and automated emails. If Business B needs to hire additional staff, the onboarding and training requirements are relatively manageable because their Standard Operating Procedure manual is up to date and includes almost everything a newbie will need to learn the ropes and excel at their job.

6.2.1 LEADERSHIP AND CULTURE

As both businesses continue to grow, leadership and culture will have a greater and greater influence on their ability to scale. After all, staff learn by observing their leaders and teammates. Esoteric values like *ambition, work ethic, innovation* and *teamwork* can mean different things to different people, which is why culture can get lost in translation very quickly when businesses are growing quickly.

Without intimate knowledge of the new owners of Business A or B, it is difficult to say with any certainty which business is better set up for scalable leadership and culture. However, generally speaking, buyers would assume Business B has a stronger chance because the previous owner had already hired a small team and established a hierarchy of roles and responsibilities within the business.

If you have an inkling that your business might benefit from operating more like Business B, then follow these steps:

1. Take stock of current systems and processes and identify any redundancies and inefficiencies that can be eliminated through free or (very) cheap software solutions.

2. Automate as many systems and processes without diluting the value of your offering to customers. Integrate as much as possible so that data collection and performance tracking are automated and easy to analyze.

3. Optimize new systems and processes to further improve operational efficiency and cohesion, and improve customer experience and lead Conversion Rates.

4. Document new and improved systems and processes in a Standard Operating Procedure (SOP) document and train your team to treat it like a living, breathing resource that needs to be updated as soon as any adjustments are made to a system or process.

5. Delegate scalable systems, processes and tasks to a contractor or junior staff member so you and the more experienced teammates can focus on growing and scaling your business further.

6.3 HOW MARKET CONDITIONS IMPACT SCALABILITY

Market conditions can also influence how easy (or

challenging) it is to scale your business. Market conditions are in constant flux and can vary considerably depending on which market you operate in. For instance, smaller niche markets present different Scalability obstacles to what larger markets typically do.

In smaller, more niche markets, where total market value falls between $1 million - $100 million, a common market factor that can hamper Scalability is *Market Saturation*. Whereas in larger markets, your ability to scale is more likely to be hampered by heavy *Market Competition* from the goliath brands that benefit from Economies of Scale (5.2.6). In both cases, businesses can find themselves bumping their head on a glass ceiling, where growth becomes difficult and they start to experience Diminishing Rates of Return.

6.3.1 DIMINISHING RATES OF RETURN

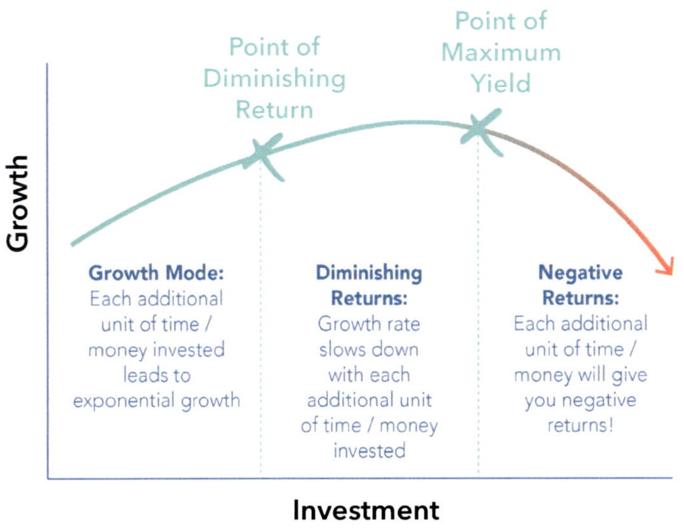

The early signs of a Scalability problem will usually manifest in the form of Diminishing Rates of Return. If you are one of the few lucky ones who gained traction and momentum soon after starting your business, then you may have experienced a linear relationship between *input* and *output*. That is to say, every additional resource unit (time, money, etc.) that you invested in your business led to greater business performance.

Alas, no matter who you are, or how great your business is, you will eventually reach a point where it becomes harder and more expensive to acquire new customers and grow your market share. In fact, you may reach a point where you have to increase your marketing spend just to *retain* your market share. This *point* is the *Point of Diminishing Returns* that you can see in the diagram above. Reaching this point is also known as experiencing *the growth problem*. For some entrepreneurs, it's the point where they might decide to raise capital to break through that infamous glass ceiling to continue scaling their business. If you're a diehard Bootstrapper like me, and raising capital is not your journey, don't try fitting a square peg in a round hole. Not always, but oftentimes, there's more than one way to skin a cat.

However, I must stress that a Diminishing Rate of Return can be like a cancerous tumor. If left undiagnosed for too long, it can kill your business. If you don't address the problem, the marginal return on your input will eventually decrease to zero, beyond which point you will start generating a negative return on your efforts, and your numbers will begin to go backwards. To avoid getting yourself into a serious pickle, be sure to regularly monitor your LTV:CAC Ratio, as well as your CAC, LTV, CLV metrics.

Of course, buyers will also be analyzing these same metrics to assess the scalability of your business. They will not only analyze the Trend of your Customer Acquisition Costs, but will also consider the conditions of the market in which your business operates to project how easily your business can be scaled and to *what extent, at what cost*.

You might still be wondering, what causes Diminishing Rates of Return in the first place? We will look at two market forces - *Market Saturation* and *Market Competition* - that are often the root cause of this common enemy.

6.3.2 MARKET SATURATION

If your business operates in a small market, you may find yourself bumping your head on a glass ceiling, where growth becomes difficult due to Market Saturation. This is particularly common in highly niche-specific markets, such as the eCommerce business we brokered in 2017 that sold specialized accessories for Dachshunds, otherwise known as Sausage Dogs. Whilst there is a surprising amount of demand for these products, the market size for sausage dog products is considerably smaller than the market size for pets of all shapes and sizes.

To demonstrate Market Saturation in action, let's compare two hypothetical online retailers that both reported an annual turnover of $4 million in the most recent financial year. One sells Sausage Dog products only and the other sells products for pets of all shapes and sizes.

Buyers will be acutely aware that the Sausage Dogs business is already dominating the Niche market and is likely on the verge of experiencing Market Saturation and Diminishing Rates of Return. In order to double the Sausage Dogs business, the buyer will have to win another 25% market share, which is likely to be much harder and more

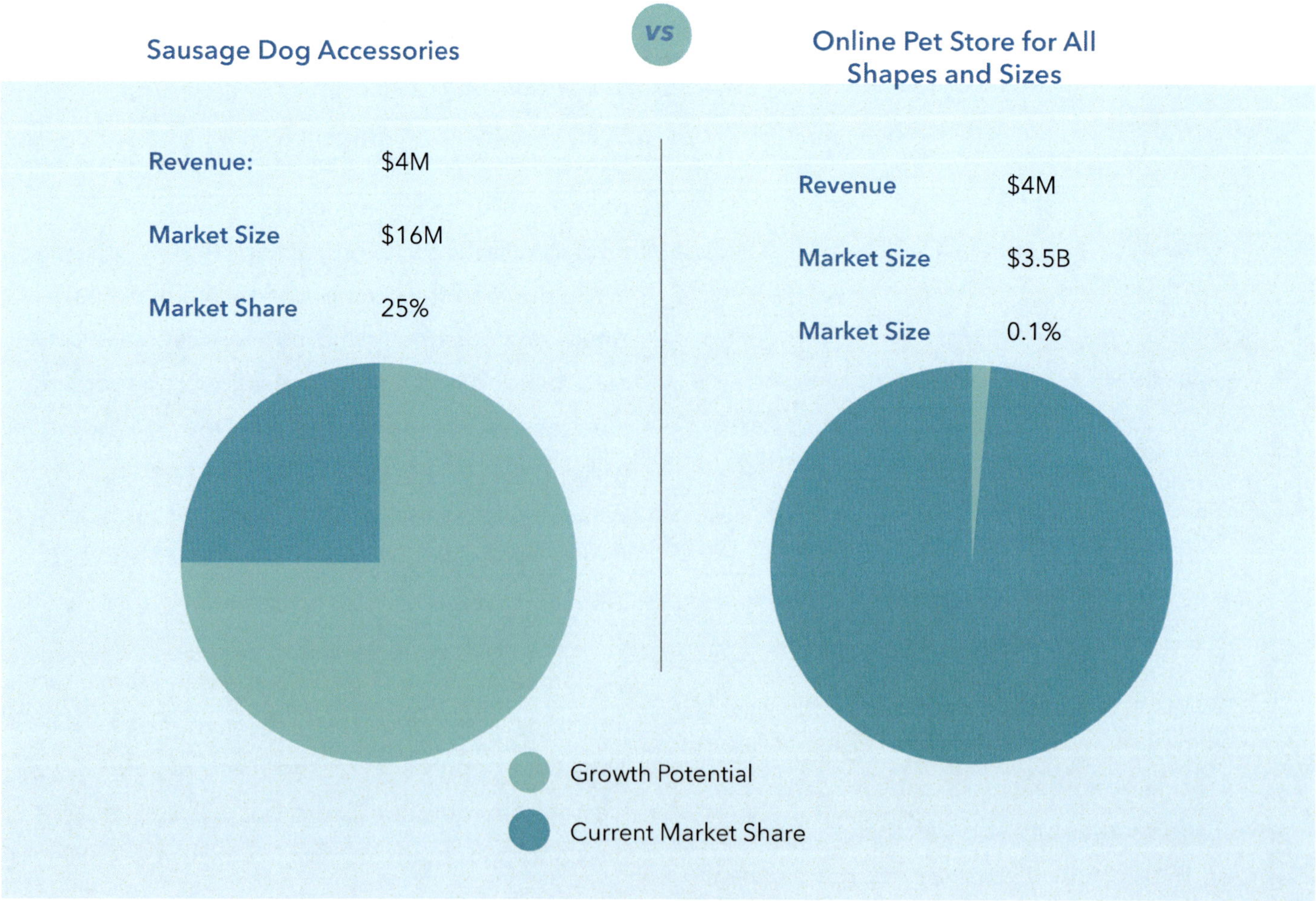

expensive to do than it was for the business to win its first 25% share. conversely, the All Pets Superstore, only has to win another 0.1% market share to double their business. Whilst Market Saturation is less common in larger markets, there is often much stiffer competition, which presents its own growth challenges.

6.3.3 MARKET COMPETITION

If your business operates in a larger market, you might find yourself bumping your head on the same glass ceiling but for another reason entirely - *competition*. Big markets usually have big players, and big players are often bullies. As you already know, it is *very* hard to win market share from the big behemoths, making it very tough to grow in this environment.

Let's consider the Email Service Provider (ESP) market, which was valued at almost $200 billion in 2020. Over the years I have worked with many clients who own ESPs that provide compelling alternatives to the likes of MailChimp and Constant Contact. These clients typically generated between $30,000 - $150,000 in monthly recurring revenue (MRR) and had a specialized offering tailored to a specific industry (e.g. real estate).

I have noticed that the glass ceiling in this market seems to be somewhere around that $150,000 MRR mark. Beyond this point, my clients seemed to experience Diminishing Rates of Return on their marketing spend. This happens because advertising keywords are expensive, and it's difficult to steal market share from competitors like Mailchimp, who spend millions (if not 10s of millions) on acquiring new customers each year. Some of our clients had to increase their marketing spend just to sustain their existing customer base, taking a hit on their bottom line. Alas, this is the harsh reality of a competitive marketplace and Economies of Scale (5.2.6).

The best way to navigate market forces and avoid a growth problem is know what to invest in and when. Investing too much in sales before expanding your product offering to meet a wider set of potential customers could bring about saturation and decreasing returns. On the other hand, over-investing in your product/service without having the marketing muscle to acquire new customers over tough competitors with deep pockets is often a losing game.

If your business scores low in Scalability, there's no need to beat yourself up about it. Many small online businesses, and certain business models in particular, score low in this area. Different from Performance and Sustainability, scoring low in Scalability won't create significant downward pressure on your Multiplier, provided the business is performing well and is sustainable. However, I can tell you that a highly scalable business will earn you significant bonus points with almost any Buyer, and will almost certainly result in a much higher Valuation.

In the following two Chapters, I'm going to get into Transferability or Auditability, which are two Value Pressures you cannot afford to ignore. Should your business score low for either Value Pressure, you can expect your Valuation to get a very drastic haircut indeed. But first, here's an activity for you to complete...

ACTIVITY 6A

Gauging Scalability Pressures

1. Refer back to 6.1 and place your business along the scalability spectrum

2. List the reasons why you placed your business there (e.g. eCommerce business model, highly competitive marketplace, etc.)

ACTIVITY 6B

Action Items

Brainstorm any aspects of your business that could be worked on to improve its scalability and overall value. Describe how it would improve scalability, what resources it would require, and the likely impact it would have on your Multiplier by taking this action.

ACTION	HOW	RESOURCES	IMPACT
E.g. Streamline operations	*Replace existing procurement system from manual data entry in excel spreadsheet to a software program that's integrated with the website and point of sales system.*	*Software subscription*	*Low to Medium*

KEY TAKEAWAYS

SCALABILITY GAUGE

- 'Scalability' is distinct from 'Growth' and is defined as the ability to which a company can grow its Revenue while maintaining or reducing its cost base.
- Some Business Models are inherently more scalable than others. SaaS and Transactional/ Marketplace businesses are typically considered the most scalable Business Models, because the cost per customer often reduces exponentially as the business grows.
- Digital product eCommerce, Subscription eCommerce and Content publishing businesses are generally scalable, again due to their ability to grow sales without necessarily having to increase cost significantly.
- Service and product-based businesses are the least scalable, as in order to grow sales, they need to increase operational costs.
- Buyers will evaluate how well your business' systems and processes have been automated, optimized, integrated, and documented in order to determine how they would respond to rapid growth. Nothing exposes weak points in a business' systems and processes better than significant growth over a short period of time.
- Buyers will also assess the leadership and culture within your work team, which can have a significant impact on a business' ability to scale.
- Market conditions, such as Market Saturation and Market Competition, can also influence how easily (or difficult) it is to scale your business. Market conditions are in constant flux and vary considerably depending on which market you operate in.
- In cases of both Market Saturation and Market Competition, businesses can often find themselves bumping their head on a glass ceiling, where growth becomes difficult and they start to experience Diminishing Rates of Return.
- Diminishing Rates of Return is where the Customer Acquisition Cost starts to increase. In other words, it becomes harder and more expensive to acquire a new customer and grow market share.
- Market Saturation is more common for businesses operating in smaller niche markets, whereas Market Competition is more likely to be a problem for businesses operating in larger markets, where it is difficult to steal market share from large competitors with multi-million dollar marketing budgets.

- Investing too much in sales before expanding your product offering to meet a wider set of potential customers could bring about saturation and decreasing returns.

- Over-investing in your product/service without the marketing muscle to support it against competitors will not generate revenue.

GAUGING TRANSFERABILITY

7

7. GAUGING TRANSFERABILITY

Transferability relates to how easily a prospective buyer can take over the ownership of your business without any disruption to its performance or operations.

Transferability Pressures create more Downward Pressure than Upward Pressure on the Multiplier

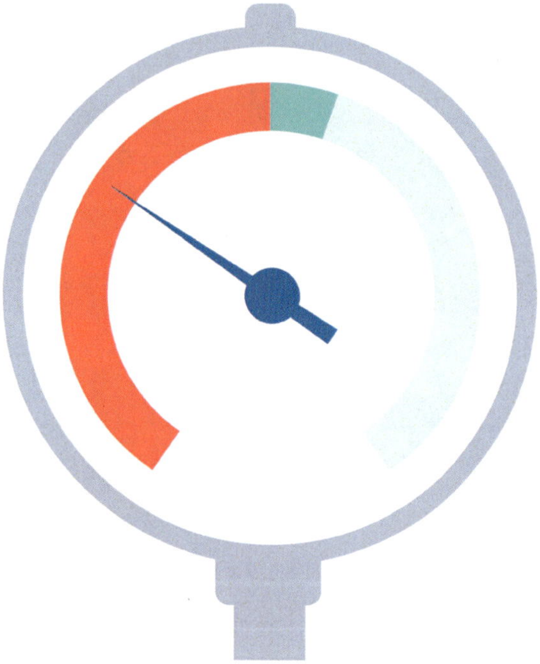

Different to Defensibility and Scalability Pressures, a highly transferable business won't necessarily create much upwards pressure on your Multiplier. However, if your business scores low in Transferability, then your Valuation will be *penalized* considerably. The reason why less transferrable businesses tend to sell for significantly lower Multipliers is because of the increased risk exposure they create for prospective acquirers.

As I've explained, the intrinsic value of your business is made up of thousands of variables, tangible and intangible, internal and external. Therefore it is almost impossible to accurately predict how the absence of a single variable will impact the future performance and value of your business. It could be inconsequential, or it could result in a significant drop in sales. This is why a seemingly insignificant asset that is difficult to transfer can intensify a Buyer's risk exposure and create Downward Pressure on your Multiplier.

So, the more transferable your business is, the more confidence a potential acquirer will have in their ability to get a return on their investment within the timeframe they anticipated. The inverse relationship between confidence and transferability is demonstrated in the diagram below.

Some business Assets are easier to transfer than others, and some may not be transferable at all. The list below is by no means exhaustive, but it gives you a sense for which Assets are typically straightforward to transfer and which Assets might require more time and consideration.

RELATIONSHIP BETWEEN BUYER CONFIDENCE & TRANSFERABILITY

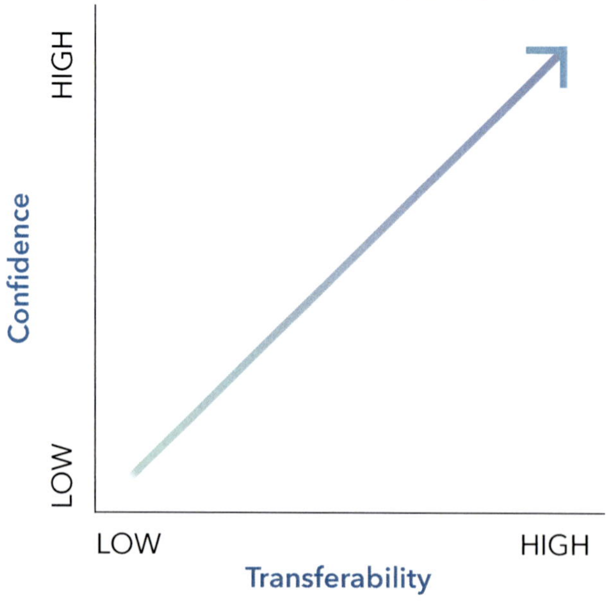

Easy	Moderate	Difficult
Domain Name	Brand Equity	Owner's Personal Brand
Web Hosting	Social Media Accounts	Owner experience, knowledge and skills
Customer Database	Payment Gateways	Leadership and Culture
Email List	Team experience, knowledge and skills	
CRM System	Customer Relationships	
Standard Operating Procedure Doc	Third-Party Relationships	
Financial Records		
Licenses, Patents and Copyrights		
Lease Agreement		

Every business is different, so you may wish to categorize the transferability of your assets differently. Now it's time to put ourselves in a Buyer's shoes and consider how transferrable some of your business Assets are.

7.1 HOW TRANSFERABLE ARE YOU?

One Asset that won't typically transfer with the sale of your business is the owner who's selling it – YOU! Ultimately, your business is worth the sum value of all your transferable Assets to someone else, *minus you*.

Some businesses are much more reliant on their owners than others. Which is to say, that if the owner suddenly vanished, some businesses would carry on unaffected, while others would be in *big, big trouble*. If the owner is closely tied to the brand and its operations, prospective buyers would consider this a significant risk, as changing ownership could result in the loss of customers and key relationships.

Some experienced Buyers will structure a deal where the owner retains a small amount of Equity in the business, so as to incentivize their continued involvement and commitment in favor of the company's future prosperity. Buyers who acquire a business outright will look to secure as much post-sale training and support from the owner as they can. Both risk mitigation techniques have been reported to be highly effective, although you can never remove the risk entirely.

Smaller owner-operated businesses have a greater tendency to be reliant on their owners. This is especially true of Digital Services businesses that survive and thrive based on interpersonal relationships. Content businesses where the owners are authoring and publishing articles themselves are equally problematic. Finally, the owner of an enterprise SaaS company responsible for developing and maintaining the code, or for onboarding and maintaining client relationships, is also cause for concern from an owner-dependency perspective. All three cases demonstrate a heavy reliance on the owner's unique experience and skillset, making it difficult for Buyers to determine the cost of replacing or forgoing this resource.

So, how transferable are YOU?

Ask yourself the following questions:

What degree of specialized knowledge is required from you to run the business?
A business that requires highly specialized knowledge from its owner will limit the number of Buyers capable of running your business. Lower demand can create Downward Pressure on the Multiplier.

What is the relationship like between you and your customers?
If you are on a first-name basis with the majority of your clients, then Buyers will be concerned that your exit may result in the exit of some of your customers, too.

For which aspects of the business are you directly responsible?
The more responsibilities you have, the more dependent your business will be on you as its operator.

What degree of leadership and management exists in the business outside of ownership?
Acquiring a business with a manager or leadership team is quite different from acquiring a business without one. Steering company culture and managing people are delicate and challenging tasks, which is why Buyers will pay a premium for a business that already has this under control.

At the end of the day, your business' value is not determined by how well *you* run the business, but by how well the business runs *without you*. The aim is to create as much distance as possible between yourself and the brand.

Here are some ways you can achieve more distance between you and your brand:

1. If you are a significant contributor to the website's content, consider creating an alias or training up a team member to write the majority of the content.

2. If you are heavily involved in the daily operations, consider hiring or promoting an employee to a leadership role, and find ways to delegate tasks to other teammates without putting too much pressure on your bottom line.

3. If your role is instrumental to your business' success, consider training someone to replace you before you depart.

4. If you communicate directly with customers and third-party providers, include a teammate and encourage them to lead the conversations and eventually take over the relationships.

5. Develop a comprehensive Standard Operating Procedure (SOP) document that you and your team can easily update and engage with.

6. Transfer any specialized knowledge or skills that you possess to existing teammates or new recruits.

Ultimately, by building a strong management team, motivated enough to stay and carry on growing the business without you, the prospects for continued prosperity are strong. After all, Buyers won't make much of your business without its 'secret recipe' for success.

7.2 HOW TRANSFERABLE IS YOUR TEAM?

Any good leader will treat their team members like they are irreplaceable. However, from a risk perspective, the less reliant your business is on a particular team member, the better. A Buyer will look to measure the impact of various staff members exiting the business by determining the time and costs required to hire and train their replacements.

When helping clients plan their exit, we encourage them to assess the knowledge, experience, and skill level of each member of their team, in order to understand how easily they can be replaced. If there is too much reliance on a particular member of your team, you may want to consider restructuring your operations to spread the specialized knowledge or responsibility (risk) throughout your team.

We also recommend implementing incentives for your teammates to continue working for the business under new ownership. For instance, you might offer your teammates a bonus payment if they continue working alongside the new owner for at least six months after the acquisition. Aligning your team's goals with your own exit goals can make the process of selling a business much easier and far less stressful.

7.3 HOW TRANSFERABLE IS YOUR OPERATING PROCEDURE?

When you buy something, it always comes with instructions, right? It doesn't matter if you buy wireless headphones or a microwave dinner - everything comes with instructions. *A business should be no different.* When assessing your business, Buyers will try to determine whether they can run it successfully, along with the time and financial investment required to do so. Therefore, having all business systems and processes compiled in a 'Standard Operating Procedure' (SOP) document will aid analysis and build significant confidence amongst Buyers.

Up-to-date SOPs make your routine systems and processes transparent, portable, and transferable to a new owner. They also provide readiness for future growth, as they ensure quality output and the continuation of set company standards when expanding the business or hiring new employees. When documenting operational tasks, it is important to accurately establish the average time you and your team members spend on completing each task.

Task	Team Member	Hours Per Week
Customer Support	Declan	30
Design & Development	Josie	15
Social Media	Mark	25
Content & SEO	Ted	20
Management & Operations	Katherine	38

Effective use of SOPs and step-by-step guidelines will ensure your company's vital processes are replicable and within reach of a potential Buyer, thus increasing your Multiplier.

7.4 HOW TRANSFERABLE ARE YOUR THIRD-PARTY ACCOUNTS?

The ability to transfer third-party accounts can have a surprisingly big impact on the Valuation of your business and the likelihood of you selling it.

When it comes to Subscription Businesses, transferring accounts can be tricky. Many subscription accounts cannot be transferred over to a new owner unless the current proprietor is selling the entire corporate entity, rather than only the business Assets. In such an event, all existing subscribers would need to subscribe again with the new owner's payment account details. This usually results in significant customer churn and, therefore, Revenue losses. Sometimes, processors will authorize a subscription transfer, but this is viewed on a case-by-case basis and it is generally the exception, not the rule.

For instance, if the Buyer cannot take over your PayPal account, they will have to contact every subscribing customer and convince them to re-subscribe to the new PayPal account. Without exception, a decent percentage of customers never re-subscribe, resulting in a significant loss of Revenue to the new owner.

Subscription Billing Platforms	Can I transfer it?
PayPal Business Account	Yes, the account is transferable.
Personal PayPal Account	No, the account is non-transferable.*
Stripe	Yes, the account is transferable.

**If you are currently charging customer subscriptions through your personal Paypal account, it is strongly recommended that you upgrade to a Paypal Business Account when preparing for the sale.*

If you own a Content business monetized through advertising or affiliate networks, you'll want to confirm directly with your network provider as to whether or not the current account can be transferred.

Advertising/Affiliate Network	Can I transfer it?
Google AdSense	No, but the Buyer can apply for a new account.
Infolinks	No, but the Buyer can apply for a new account.
AdRoll	No, but the Buyer can apply for a new account.
Amazon Associates	No, but the Buyer can apply for a new account.

Note: These are subject to change and can often vary depending on where your business is based. Although the account itself cannot be transferred, most ad networks are more than happy to pre-approve a new owner for an account if notified in advance.

Transactional Platforms like Amazon, eBay, Envato, and Etsy do not always make it easy to transfer accounts from one owner to another. In fact, the majority don't accommodate the account transfer option, and those who do usually have strict terms and requirements in place.

As we can see from the table on the following page, not all Revenue streams are transferable to a new owner. Therefore, it is essential to contact your

Transactional Platforms	Can you transfer it?
Shopify	Yes, the account is transferable.
Amazon FBA*	Yes, the account is transferable.
Merch by Amazon	No, the account is non-transferable.
eBay Account	No, the account is non-transferable.
Etsy Account	No, the account is non-transferable.
Envato	Yes, the account is transferable.

These are subject to change and can often vary depending on where your business is based.
**According to the Terms of Service, an Amazon account is 'generally' not transferable. However, it is in fact possible, and Amazon will allow the transfer as long as it is done in a non-disruptive way. The process can be tremendously streamlined by working with an online business broker and a qualified contract attorney.*

payment processors or any third parties involved and confirm Transferability prior to listing your business for sale.

Alternatively, the process can be streamlined significantly by working with experienced advisors and brokers, who are familiar with such situations and often have workarounds for overcoming Transferability obstacles. A professional with extensive experience in transferring online business accounts can help you figure out the right steps, remove any barriers, and verify exactly what is required for achieving an effective account transfer.

Potential Buyers will need to know all the details about the successful transfer of any accounts upfront, and by assuring them that you have appointed a qualified online business broker to facilitate the process will give both parties considerable peace of mind.

7.5 HOW TRANSFERABLE ARE THIRD-PARTY RELATIONSHIPS?

Third-party relationships include suppliers, promotional partners, vendors, contractors, service providers, and licensing agreements. These relationships can often be instrumental to the business' success, and therefore, Buyers will want to make sure that they won't be affected by the new ownership.

Your business may benefit from discounted supplier rates or an above-average affiliate payout rate, thus contributing to its high-level performance. You might have also agreed upon special pricing with your contractors, or favorable terms from your service providers. However, don't expect that prospective Buyers will be comfortable with gentleman's agreements. If you can't get a written guarantee that these favorable terms will be honored under new ownership, Buyers will consider the risk of these relationships changing and how that could impact business performance and their rate of return.

Here's an example of a reasonable risk a buyer will want to be protected from when acquiring your business: let's pretend your SaaS business benefits from Grandfather Pricing where you get extremely cheap hosting because you were one of the hosting company's first customers back in 2010. Your monthly hosting bill is only $100/month but other customers who are on the same data plan as your business pay $1,000/month. Your business saves $900 a month and $10,800 a year. A Buyer will want to know whether or not your business will continue to benefit from Grandfather Pricing under their ownership. Without a written agreement in place, there is no guarantee, exposing them to a potential unforseen increase in operating cost that could reduce their rate of return. This considered, I strongly recommend you to obtain written agreements with all critical stakeholders that ensure the current relationship will be honored under new ownership.

To maximize your Transferability score, consider how transferrable your business *truly* is, and what you can do to make it more transferrable.

- How well have you detached your personal brand from your business brand?
- To what extent have you disseminated your winning formula throughout your business?
- Will your team continue with the business under new ownership?
- Is there a high level of dependency on any particular team member?
- Do you have any team incentive plan in place that will aid you in the exit of your business?
- Can you transfer your third-party accounts?
- Do you have written agreements in place that ensure key relationships will continue as is?
- Have you documented your standard operating procedures to create transparency and build confidence?

If your departure from your business will be '*business as usual*', then Multiplier will be largely impacted and may even slightly improve. On the contrary, if your departure is a catalyst for customer churn, the loss of team members or key partnerships, then your Multiplier is likely to shrink quite considerably. Before listing your business for sale, make sure you have removed as many Transferability obstacles as possible, in order to avoid any dip in value.

ACTIVITY 7A

Gauging Transferability Pressures

Step One: Divide your assets into two lists, those that are transferable and those that are not. Highlight any assets that cannot be included that are likely to create Downward Pressure on your Multiplier. The easiest way to identify these assets is to ask yourself whether a cautious buyer would have any reason to question the future performance of the business in the absence of that asset. For instance, keeping your personal laptop will not have any negative impact, but not being able to transfer a personal Paypal account for a subscription business will.

Step Two: Determine whether each Transferability aspect of your business creates Upward, Downward or Neutral pressure on the Multiplier (you can use the table on the following page as a starting point).

1. Score the likely impact this pressure will have on your Multiplier out of 3 (1 or -1 = small impact, 2 or -2 = big impact, 3 or -3 = huge impact)

2. Calculate the total pressure applied to your Multiplier

    a. Sum of Upward Pressure impact points (e.g. 5)

    b. Sum of Downward Pressure impact points (e.g -3)

    c. Subtract Downward Pressure impact points from Upward Pressure impact points (5-3 = 2)

If you're feeling unsure about how a particular aspect of your performance will impact your Multiplier, refer to the content above, talk to a friend, or an advisor, and of course there's always Google.

3. Calculate your pressure total by summing all the impact scores.

	PRESSURE	IMPACT
How transferable (replaceable) are you?	↑ Upward Pressure ↓ Downward Pressure ~ Neutral Pressure	*E.g. -2*
How transferable is your team?		
How transferable are your operations?		
How transferable are your 3rd party accounts?		
How transferable are your 3rd party relationships?		
	TOTAL PRESSURE =	

ACTIVITY 7B

Action Items

Brainstorm any aspects of your business that could be worked on to improve its Transferability and overall value. Describe how it would improve Transferability, what resources it would require, and the likely impact it would have on your Multiplier by taking this action. Even if you're feeling unsure about some of your ideas, write them down anyway. Remember, this is just an exercise.

ACTION	HOW	RESOURCES	IMPACT
E.g. Reduce business' dependency on me	*Promote team member to leadership position*	*Training and support*	*High*

KEY TAKEAWAYS

TRANSFERABILITY GAUGE

- Transferability relates to how easily a prospective Buyer can take over the ownership of your business without major disruption to its performance or operations.
- Business value is not determined by how well *you* run your business, but rather by how well it runs *without you*.
- The more Transferable your business is, the more confident potential buyers will be in their ability to maintain and grow your business.
- Consider how Transferable the follows aspects of your business are:
- Owner Dependency: Ultimately, your business is worth the sum value of all your transferable Assets to someone else, *minus you*.
- Will your departure be 'business as usual' or the catalyst for customer churn and the loss of team members or key partnerships?
- How closely tied is your personal brand tied to your business brand?
- What degree of specialized knowledge is required from you or co-owners to successfully run your business?
- Team Leadership and Culture: Businesses that come with a well-trained team, leadership and productive work culture garner a lot of interest in the market for two reasons: (i) it reduces the risk and complexity of taking over a business, and (ii) training people as well as cultivating leadership and culture requires a lot of hard work over a long period of time.
- Will your team continue working under new ownership?
- Are there any leaders in your team aside from the owners?
- Is your business too heavily dependent on a single team member?

- Standard Operating Procedures: When you buy something, it always comes with instructions, right? A business should be no different. Comprehensive documentation of your Standard Operating Procedures (SOP) will radically improve the Transferability of your business. Most importantly, it creates transparency and builds confidence in a Buyers' ability to run your business.

- Third-Party Accounts: Not all business accounts are transferable, so spend some time establishing which ones are, which ones are not, and what the possible solutions are. List all of your third-party accounts; social media, payment gateways, advertising/affiliate networks, marketplaces, and other transactional platforms.

- Third-Party Relationships: Make sure that all your business' relationships with suppliers, promotional partners, vendors, contractors, other partnerships, etc., will continue under new ownership. The only way to guarantee this and put Buyers' minds at ease is to obtain written agreements in place that transfer with the business so they still apply under new ownership.

GAUGING AUDITABILITY

8

8. GAUGING AUDITABILITY

Auditability is measured by a Buyer's ability to verify everything you claim about your business. Similar to Transferability, a highly verifiable business won't typically add Upward Pressure on your Multiplier, but if you're unable to verify business performance to a reasonable degree, you can expect a much lower sale price. And if you're unable to verify your business at all, it will be impossible to sell all together.

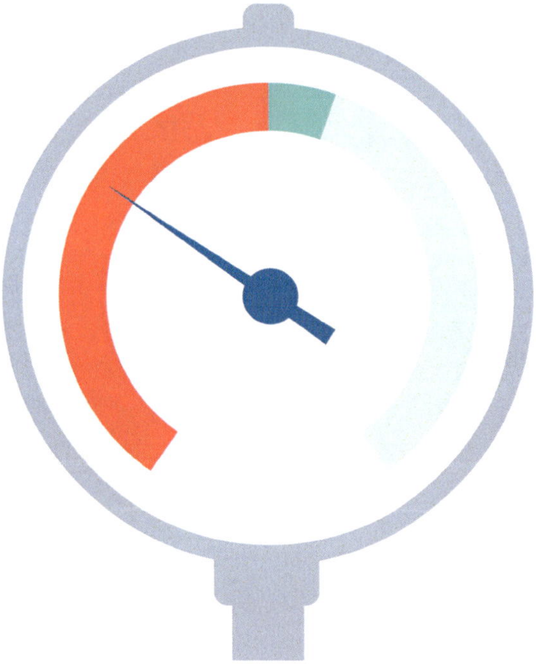

Auditability Pressures create more Downward Pressure than Upward Pressure on the Multiplier

If you are still unconvinced of the importance of Auditability, here are three reasons that should drive it home:

1. **We all make mistakes.** I'll be the first to admit that I have, in the past, recorded information incorrectly, misinterpreted data, and bungled the installation of performance tracking tools. Although these are all honest mistakes, any misinformation could have a major impact on a Buyer's expected ROI.

2. **It's the wild, wild west.** Buying and selling online businesses over the internet with the absence of eye contact and a handshake can tempt some people into engaging in fraudulent behavior. Although you might feel like you are trustworthy, Buyers can (and should) only trust comprehensive, verifiable information.

3. **Well-oiled machines sell well.** A business that is easy to Audit and verify is often well-built, well-organized and easy to operate. Naturally, Buyers will prefer to take over a well-oiled machine as opposed to a clunky one riddled with hidden surprises.

When you list a business for sale, you will need to create a *Sales Prospectus* detailing all the key information about your business. The more comprehensive the prospectus, the fewer annoying questions you will have to answer *over and over again*. A good prospectus will include an overview of the Business Model and operations, a list of included Assets, financial data, Traffic data and other key performance Metrics.

Seriously interested buyers will want to verify everything in your prospectus and more. Out of the many hundreds of businesses I've worked with over the years, I have recommended the overwhelming majority of them to improve their Auditability in preparation for sale.

There are two underpinning principles to improving Auditability:

1 Clean data.

Avoid the temptation of mixing data from other businesses and your personal life. Although you can save time and money when starting up a new business through the existing entity or paying for personal Expenses through the business account, it can be very difficult and sometimes impossible to detangle the commingled data and therefore fully verify financial performance.

2 Third-Party Validation.

The more third-party data you have to validate your claims, the more confidence Buyers will have in you and your business. A financial report with only bank statements as supporting evidence is very different to also having tax returns, Merchant accounts and 3rd party sales reports.

8.1 AUDITING FINANCIALS

When Buyers conduct an Audit of your financials, they are trying to protect themselves against two things:

1. **Inflated revenue.** Buyers will verify income statements against bank statements and tax returns to verify that the revenue adds up. They will also analyze your customer database and sales records to make sure that the reported revenue is being generated through sales of the business that you are selling, and not some other business.
2. **Undisclosed Expenses.** Buyers will use tax returns to verify the operational cost of a business. Tax returns are generally the best source for uncovering undisclosed Expenses because business owners are incentivized to report any and all business Expenses in order to reduce their tax Liability.

I have seen deals fall through at the 11th hour because the Buyer can't verify the financials to their satisfaction. We have also seen clients breeze through the sales process without a hitch because their clean books instilled confidence in the Buyer. Below are some tips that will ensure your financial performance is easily verifiable:

1. **Detangle commingled accounts.** Separate any shared accounts so that your business has standalone accounts for all business-specific transactions. I know it's a pain in the backside, but it's very difficult -- and sometimes impossible -- to do this when you're midway through the sales process. If you decide it's too much bother, you need to be prepared for a lower Valuation and a potentially disappointing exit. Speak with an advisor for more insight on your particular situation.
2. **Install accounting software.** Solutions like Quickbooks and Xero will not only save you time, but they will also win you bonus points with Buyers because they are familiar with the accounting systems and reporting methods. Familiarity equates to confidence.
3. **Categorize transactions accurately.** If you label transactions precisely and consistently, it will allow buyers to breeze through their financial

Audit. If you cut corners and lump Expenses into generic categories like "sales", "software", and "marketing", then it will be difficult for buyers to get a detailed picture of how you are operating your business. Subcategories also make it easier to add back any one-time or unnecessary Expenses when calculating the Seller's Discretionary Earnings (SDE).

4. **Build a paper trail.** As mentioned earlier, the more third-party data you have to substantiate your financial performance claims, the better. Ideally, all of these reports will complement and validate one another to build a solid paper trail. In cases where discrepancies between reports are unavoidable, make sure they are explainable and that your explanation can be verified. Here's a checklist:

   ✓ TTM Profit & Loss Statement (monthly breakdown)

   ✓ Historial Profit & Loss Statements

   ✓ Tax returns

   ✓ Monthly bank statements

   ✓ Payment gateway reports

8.2. AUDITING TRAFFIC AND CUSTOMERS

Buyers will look to verify the performance of your business by auditing your website Traffic and customer data. In Chaprer 3, we learned how various performance Metrics influence your Valuation. For instance, if your business is reporting a low customer Churn Rate or high Customer Lifetime Value, then Buyers will want to verify that this is accurate. Tracking performance via Third-Party Platforms is the easiest and most comprehensive way for you, valuers, and prospective Buyers to verify key Metrics.

8.2.1 AUDITING TRAFFIC DATA

It is just as important to have Google Analytics installed on your website as it is to have bank statements, because they are both considered a bare minimum requirement from Brokers and Buyers alike. While some Buyers will accept just 12 months of data, many will expect to see Traffic data dating back to the inception of your business.

It is also essential to ensure that Google Analytics tracking codes are not installed twice on the same site, distorting data and reporting abnormally low bounce rates and high Traffic volumes. If you are concerned this might be the case, there are a number of online resources that can help you to confirm this and fix the problem. Alternatively, you can contact Google or reach out to someone who is digitally savvy in your network.

8.2.2 AUDITING CUSTOMER DATA

eCommerce platforms like Shopify and SaaS platforms like Chart Mogul will help you track key customer Metrics like Average Order Value or Churn Rate. Buyers tend to trust these Third-Party Platforms because they have no incentive to deliberately fudge the figures. However, these analytics platforms are only as accurate as the information you feed them, which is why some Buyers will crunch the raw customer sales data as a fail-safe cross check.

If you don't currently use a customer analytics platform specific to your Business Model, it is highly recommended you start using one right away. On top of making your business more auditable and verifiable, it will also help you to make more informed business decisions.

8.3 AUDITING OPERATIONS

Anyone who has been buying and selling online businesses long enough will know that the most easily misrepresented aspect of any business is its operations. This is because financial, Traffic and customer data can be verified by raw data inputs, whereas verifying operations is much less black and white.

When Buyers assess your business, they will try to determine the time and subsequent cost it will take for them to run it successfully themselves. As we touched on in 2.4, the more hours it takes a Buyer to run the acquired business in order to generate an ROI, the lower his or her hourly rate becomes. Consciously or subconsciously aware of the fact that this drives the business' value down, many owners claim to spend fewer hours per week on their business than what they really do.

	What Owner Says	vs	The Reality
Managing Staff	1 hr / week		8 hrs / week
Accounting	1 hr / month		2 hrs / week
Marketing	1 hr / week		3 hrs / week
Customer Support	2 hrs / week		8 hrs / week

This tendency to understate their involvement is not so much a deliberate lie, but more so, a skewed recollection of their reality. When an owner is preparing to exit their business, they are acutely aware that a passive investment is far more attractive to most Buyers than a time-intensive one. Subconsciously, owners have a propensity to say to themselves, "*Someone could do my job in an hour a day if they outsourced some tasks and are really focused*." They might also imagine a perfect week where everything runs smoothly without a hitch and say to themselves, "*Five hours a week is all you need*." If you continue to imagine what you want to see, you start to see a mirage. Unfortunately, Buyers won't see what you see, and they'll want proof to substantiate your claims.

Another common misrepresentation made by owners is the skills and knowledge required to successfully operate their business. This is yet another area where timesheets and a Standard Operating Procedure (SOP) are crucial, as it provides a detailed account of the systems, processes and operational tasks, enabling the buyer to determine what skills, knowledge and resources will be required to operate the business under their ownership.

TIP: Implement a time tracking / management tool to track the time you and your teammates spend on various business-related activities.

ACTIVITY 8

Gauging Auditability

Of all the Value Pressures, I find Auditability to be the easiest to influence. All you need to do is make every aspect of your business easy to verify.

Step One: Comb through this chapter and place your financials, web traffic data, customer data, and operations into three categories; 100% Verifiable, Not 100% verifiable, Unsure.

	100% VERIFIABLE	NOT 100% VERIFIABLE	UNSURE
Financials (P&L, tax returns, bank statements, etc.)			
Web Traffic (Google Analytics)			
Customer Data (database)			
Operations (SOP)			

Step Two: highlight everything that is not 100% verifiable, or you are unsure about, and create an action plan to make these aspects of your business easily verifiable. You may need to contact an accountant, advisor, or someone who's tech-savvy for some assistance. I know it's an effort, but trust me it's well worth your time.

KEY TAKEAWAYS

AUDITABILITY GAUGE

- Auditability is measured by a Buyer's ability to verify everything you claim about your business:
    - Financial Performance
    - Traffic and customers
    - Operations

- The more verifiable your business is, the more protected Buyers are from misinformation and fraud. Greater Buyer confidence will typically place upwards pressure on your Multiplier.

- You can improve the Auditability of your business by having clean data and any additional third-party validations you might be able to provide.

- **Financial Performance:** When auditing your financials, buyers will look to verify that revenue is not inflated and there are no undisclosed expenses. Here are a few tips to improve financial Auditability:
    - Detangle commingled accounts
    - Install accounting software
    - Categorize revenue and expense transactions properly
    - Build a paper trail (financial reports, Third-Party Platform validation, etc.)

- **Traffic & Customers:** Buyers will also look to verify your website Traffic and customer data to evaluate Performance, Sustainability, Defensibility and Scalability Drivers. Third-party customer analytics platforms (Google Analytics, Shopify, ChartMogul, MailChimp) are the easiest and most comprehensive way for verifying key Metrics.

- **Operations:** Anyone who has been in the game of buying and selling online businesses long enough will know that the most easily misrepresented aspect of any business is its operations. This is because financial, Traffic and customer data can be verified by raw data inputs, whereas verifying operations is much less black and white. Here are a few tips to improve the Auditability of your operations:
    - Document Standard Operating Procedures (SOPs)
    - Track the time you, any co-owners, as well as employees and contractors spend on the business each week.

MISCELLANEOUS PRESSURE GAUGES

9. MISCELLANEOUS PRESSURE GAUGES

There are a number of miscellaneous drivers of value that aren't fully captured in the seven Pressure Gauges covered so far that are deserving of our attention. I've compiled them all into this final chapter that should round out everything else you've learned in this book. Let's dive in.

9.1 MARKET NICHE

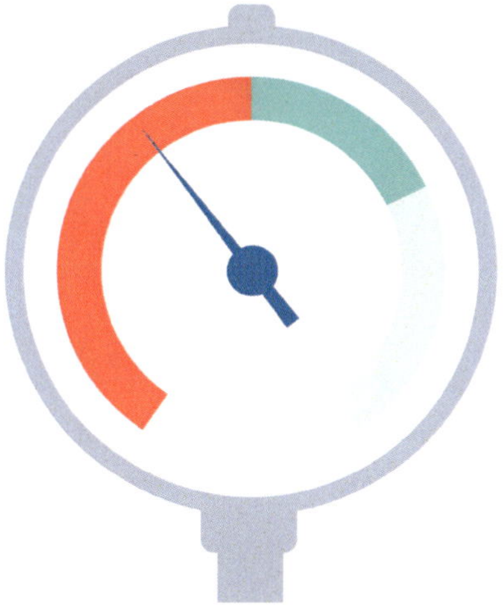

Creates significant pressure in both directions, although slightly more on the negative side

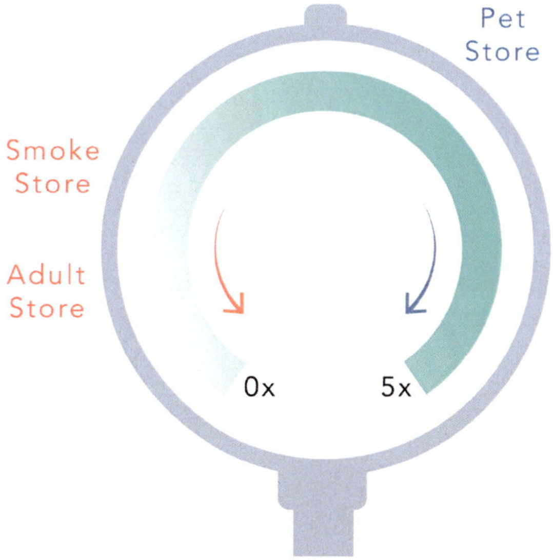

Naturally, some market niches are more sought after than others. Some niches are popular because they are on-trend, evergreen or simply valued higher in the broader community. Whereas other niches are less popular because they are off-trend or considered less socially acceptable. For instance, a pet-care products store is likely to attract more prospective Buyers than a store selling smoke paraphernalia or adult toys. As you well know by now, higher demand places Upward Pressure on the Multiplier.

9.2 RECENT CHANGES

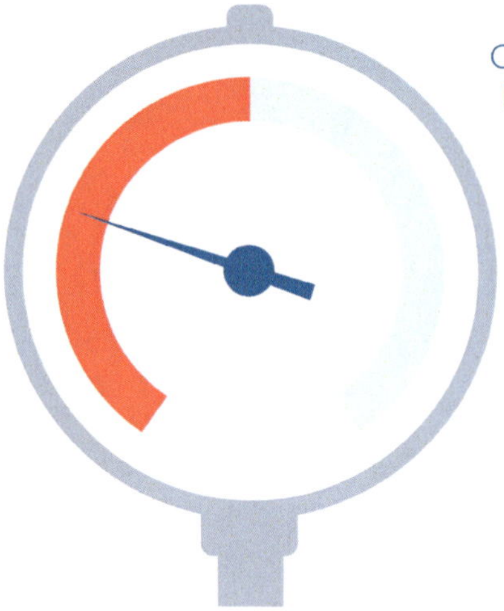

Have you made any recent changes to your business' product offering, pricing, operations, sales, or marketing activities? Recent changes can only reduce your valuation, so my advice to clients has always been to resist the temptation to make any changes to their business for at least six months prior to sale.

It's common for entrepreneurs to test new monetization methods and growth strategies. However, in the eyes of a Buyer, change means *risk*. And since Buyers look to minimize *risk*, they wouldn't rely on sporadic sales from newly implemented strategies untested by time.

If you recently lowered your prices, you might have received an increase in sales, indicating a successful outcome. However, Buyers may question the long-term impact of this decision on the business' brand and market positioning. Likewise, if there was a spike in Earnings due to increased media attention from a successful PR campaign, Buyers are aware that such major endorsements are difficult to replicate and will interpret the revenue injection with a grain of salt.

Furthermore, if you owned a content site and switched ad network providers, you would want to allow a sufficient amount of time to prove that the new ad network performs as well (or better) than the previous one. Last but not least, if you want to fatten your Profits prior to sale by reducing headcount in your business, you'll want to allow enough time to lapse to prove to Buyers that the business can sustain current performance with less staff.

The ideal business should demonstrate stability in its revenue, pricing, operations, and marketing strategies, allowing Buyers to make reasonable predictions. The more unstable the business, the harder it is for the Buyer to forecast future growth and discern their likely ROI.

> **TIP:** Don't make any significant changes to your business for at least six months prior to selling.

9.3 SEASONALITY

Although some Buyers might find the idea of working only several months per year attractive, more often than not, Seasonality has a negative impact on the Multiplier. Most Buyers prefer businesses with stable Cash Flows because this allows for easier planning and forecasting.

It is normal for sales to ebb and flow throughout the year, and of course, minor seasonality will not have an adverse effect on your Multiplier. However, highly seasonal businesses, such as an online store selling Christmas ornaments, can expect to see a minor to substantial downward pressure exerted on their Multiplier. Generally speaking, the more extreme the Seasonality, the greater impact it will have.

9.4 LIABILITY

Liability translates to a business' financial obligation to another entity arising from its implication in past events or transactions. Put simply, an inherent Liability is a ticking time bomb that could result in an outflow of resources, thus increasing the risk factor for the Buyer. Liability concerns may include data and security breaches, product misinformation, copyright infringement, fabricated reviews, and so on. Depending on the circumstances, obvious Liability matters may affect the market value of your business considerably.

9.5 INFRINGEMENTS

Is your business guilty of any infringements? If so, it may cost your Valuation dearly. Infringement occurs when a business uses another party's exclusive intellectual property (IP) – patents, copyrights, trademarks, and trade secrets – without permission. Unless expiry dates have passed or IP rights have been granted, the business is not allowed to use them in any way. Similarly, IP infringement can occur within licensing agreements.

For example, if the licensee uses the IP in a way that was not specifically defined in the scope of the licensing agreement, then they are in breach of said agreement. Intellectual property litigation can be complex, costly and time-consuming. Legal implications for the infringer include penalties, covering damages and Profit losses, paying all attorney fees and court costs, temporary cessation of business activity, and even jail time – not to mention the damage to the business' brand and reputation.

Naturally, an infringement Liability is something that Buyers will consider to be a big risk, and therefore the Multiplier can be adversely affected by the degree to which the business may be subject to a third-party infringement claim. As we mentioned in 5.2.4, IP is a valuable Asset and Defense Barrier that owners can use to boost their business' value. However, if a patent or copyright is the subject of a legal proceeding or a warning letter from a third party, the resulting red flag would create a cloud of uncertainty for the Buyer. Depending on the nature of the infringement claim, the value of the Asset could be brought into question, while the business' value would certainly diminish.

9.6 LICENSING

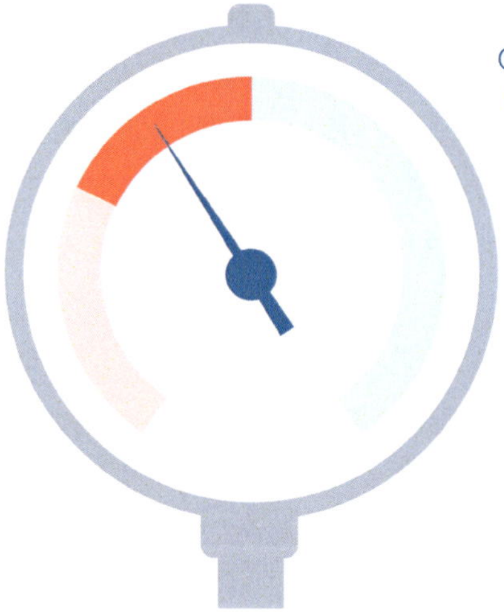

Just like their brick-and-mortar counterparts, most online businesses must follow license or permit requirements in order to operate. From mortgage lenders to eCommerce sites, legal requirements apply to all online industries, and vary depending on the nature and location of your business. In most cases, you are legally obliged to ensure that you have the appropriate – and often costly – licenses for a software that is installed on your system, as well as User or seller permits to do business within a marketplace.

Generally speaking, any license terms that would complicate the acquisition process by creating Transferability barriers and steep learning curves could negatively impact the Multiplier. If your business requires the new owner to obtain a certain license, this will result in additional time and Expenses for the Buyer.

This usually results in less demand and sometimes a lower Valuation. However, this is not a major deterrent for a strategic Buyer who already possesses this license. Furthermore, a wise owner can leverage the license obstacles to add value instead, as these deterrents also act as a Defense Barrier for the business.

9.7 CHANGING LAWS AND MARKET REGULATIONS

Changes in market regulation laws occur frequently, and one may affect your business. This is especially common within new industries and emerging market niches, whose futures are still being weighted by courts or relevant administrative bodies. Such was the case with the e-cigarette industry, whose fate was in doubt before the FDA and National courts had given their official approval.

Eventually, vaping products became successfully commercial, but not before many owners sought to sell their e-cigarette businesses in fear of their prohibition. Pending laws and regulations inevitably create a feeling of uncertainty about the future viability of a business or industry, which translates directly to risk for potential Buyers. Similarly, a business that hasn't updated its operations to fully comply with new laws, rules, and standards will experience a downward pressure on its Multiplier, as this only creates more skepticism among Buyers.

TIP: It is important to set Google Alerts to track governmental websites, so as to ensure you're always up to date. A few examples of such websites are: www.govtrack.us www.ftc.gov www.sec.gov www.fda.gov

9.8 THIRD-PARTY COMPLIANCE

The business must comply with any third-party obligations as per any terms and conditions the business, or anyone representing the business, has agreed to. Failing to do so can create an enormous amount of risk for potential acquirers. For example, an eCommerce Merchant who, knowingly or unknowingly, sells products in violation of its payment processor's terms runs a serious risk of getting their operations suspended.If you are partnering with third-party vendors, it's important to establish a robust and proactive compliance program, by regularly conducting compliance and risk assessments to avoid potential sanctions.

9.9 LEGAL DISPUTES

Legal Disputes can create unwanted risk, uncertainty and complexity for a business and its prospective Buyers. This is a relatively rare, but potentially strong, factor that can negatively impact the Multiplier. If a business comes with unresolved commercial disputes or liabilities, their settlement would divert valuable time and resources away from productive and profitable activities.

The best course of action for a business owner is to detail any current or past legal problems – including litigation, disputes, and judgments – and build a factual story with as much information as possible. This will help in understanding the limitations, liabilities, and warranties that can or cannot be agreed to, and how they apply to a company Asset sale vs. a company stock sale. The value will be affected depending on how these prior legal issues will impact the future of the business. As such, you can expect there to be heavy downward pressure on your Multiplier if your business has obvious Liability concerns.

9.10 NON-COMPETITION

Sellers are generally expected to sign a non-compete agreement as part of the sale and purchase agreement. These covenants restrict the seller from competing with the business they have sold to the Buyer for a specified period of time, typically three to five years. The seller may also be more broadly restricted from working for a business, or operating a business, in a specific industry and geographic area during this time period as well.

In any case, non-compete agreements give Buyers a certain measure of comfort and peace of mind, by ensuring that the projected Revenue streams of the purchased business will not be jeopardized by competition from the former owner. This agreement represents a promise to the Buyer that may carry significant value with regard to preserving and materializing the business' future earning potential, while minimizing risk.

Afterall, there have been occasions where competition from previous owners who didn't sign a non-compete prevented the acquirer from achieving their anticipated return on investment. Therefore, the degree to which you are willing to sign a non-compete can impact the Multiplier considerably.

9.11 EXIT MOTIVATIONS

Despite being a miscellaneous Value Pressure in our last Chapter, Exit Motivations are usually the first thing a Buyer will ask about. Nearly every acquisition begins with the seller being asked, *"Why are you selling your business?"*

This is because Buyers want to fully understand what they are getting themselves into. If a business is good enough to attract their interest, then why would any owner in their right mind give up a well-performing, easy-to-operate business that generates solid income? Afterall, for many owners, their business represents the culmination of their life's work and primary source of income. So if your business generates significant Earnings and requires just 15 hours a week to run it, be prepared to explain your Exit Motivations to interested parties.

Naturally, the reasons and factors leading to entrepreneurial exit vary widely, and not all of them will make sense to prospective Buyers. Some reasons might be completely personal, such as retirement, illness, partner disputes, or the desire to clear headspace and explore new opportunities. But the truth of the matter is that sellers do not always give the actual reasons for wanting to exit, when the *real* motivations for exiting are less straightforward. This tendency is not necessarily born from malicious intent, but rather out of fear that the Buyer could lose interest if they were to learn the real motivation for their exit. For example, there could be a decline in Revenue, upcoming negative changes in regulations, pessimistic industry Trends, or feeling burnt out and unsure how to grow the business further.

In their pursuit to detect underlying risks, purchasers will look beyond your Exit Motivations in order to identify areas of the business that may be a struggle. They will try to determine if you know something that they don't know. If your reasons seem too unconvincing or suspicious, Buyers may choose not to pursue the business due to the risk of the unknown. Ultimately, your Exit Motivations shouldn't have a significant impact on your Multiplier unless you are aware of an obvious threat that will affect the business.

9.12 OWNER PROFILE

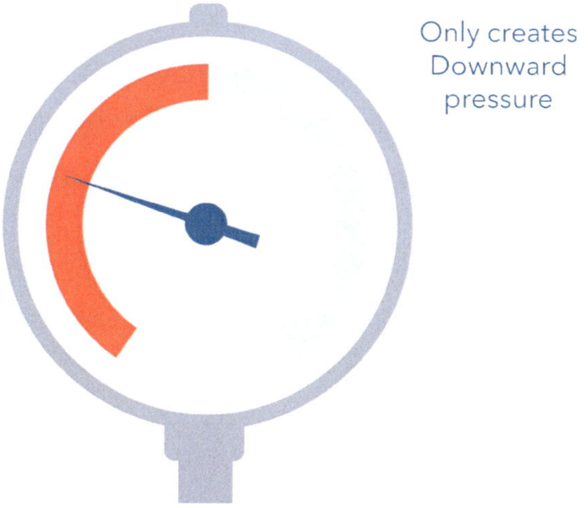

Don't freak out, but some Buyers will run a background check on you. You must understand that buying a business is equally as scary as selling one, if not more so. The seller knows what they're selling, but a buyer can never know *exactly* what they are buying – *or who they are buying it from*. When a Buyer conducts a background check on you, it is likely part of their standard due diligence process, to verify that you don't have a bad reputation for selling people dodgy businesses or any other fraudulent behavior.

If Buyers can't find you on the internet, they might assume the worst. We always recommend our clients to update their social media profiles and adjust their privacy settings, so the Buyer can get an accurate story of your career path, as well as a good idea of who you are.It is also recommended that you use tools like reputation.com or Google's 'Me on the web' to monitor what is being said about you and your brand. If there is negative or unwanted content connected with your identity, consider ethical and legitimate ways of combating this image and offering an alternative identity (4.1).

9.13 LEADERSHIP AND CULTURE

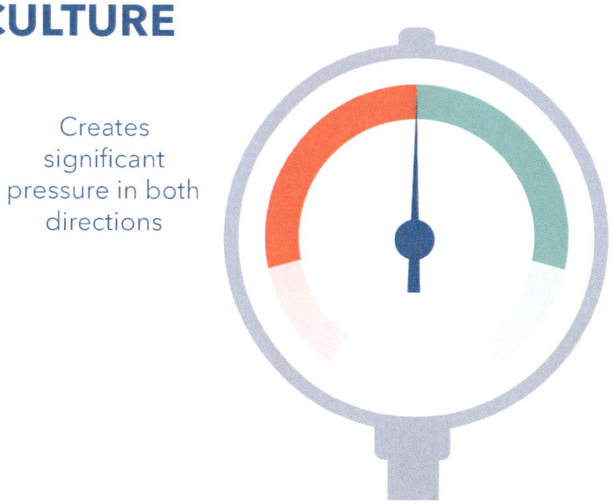

Intial Buyers may use any means to complement existing financial and intangible analysis by gaining a more thorough understanding of the business' Leadership and Culture puzzle. Since these Pressures cannot be measured by any metric or index, most will go beyond their *'gut feel'* approach and isolated observations to get a deeper insight. A rigorous evaluation may include the Leadership team's personal qualities (traits, competencies, characteristics), and the application of organization systems they have created to manage leadership throughout the business.

Such elements will be assessed in interviews, observations, surveys, reviews and reports. Potential Buyers may also run background checks on websites like Glassdoor.com to ensure that the company culture is not corrosive. Bad reviews from ex-employees could imply that the management is difficult, or that the business tolerates unethical behavior, thus damaging its reputation and suggesting a risk factor.

With strong Leadership and a vibrant productive work culture in place, Buyers are more confident in the company's future Performance, Sustainability, Scalability and Transferability, which will therefore lead to a higher Multiplier.

9.14 CONCENTRATION

Creates more Downward pressure than Upward pressure

Enquiring about a business' customer concentration is standard procedure in the Valuation process. Buyers will want to ensure that there isn't a Concentration of sales limited to a certain number of customers. If the company relies on a single or a handful of key clients to generate income, this will likely be viewed as a major risk to the business' future and a potential Buyer's ROI. If those relationships and contracts were to terminate or not transfer along with the new ownership, their loss could potentially be detrimental to the business.

Naturally, this kind of risk would apply severe downward pressure to the Multiplier and reduce the business' value. Red flags include a single customer accounting for more than 20% of Revenue, or a small customer pool accounting for more than 40% of Revenue. Inversely, a larger and more diverse customer base helps insulate a business against Revenue shortfalls due to customer loss, and can therefore contribute to a slight improvement to the Multiplier.

In a similar manner, relying too much on a few key suppliers puts the business at significant risk, by relying heavily on their decisions, policies, and goals. Vendor concentration is an element that applies mostly to eCommerce and lead generation businesses, rather than SaaS, Subscription or Content models. The potential risks that arise with vendor concentration can affect the business' performance and stability. For example, if your single primary vendor decides to raise prices, change policies, or shut down, this would create major disruptions in your business' ability to fulfill orders, stock inventory, retain Scalability levels, and so on.

Likewise, if that vendor decides to go into direct

retail and compete within your industry with the same products, they will likely do so at more competitive prices, and by using the sales data harvested from you and other clients. Hence, diversifying your vendor base can help protect your business if a supplier decides to make radical changes. That being said, a mitigating factor in vendor concentration cases would be an easily replaceable vendor. If there are plenty of alternative options offering similar policies and prices, then the negative impact on the Multiplier would be limited. Bottomline, the downward pressure on the Multiplier from vendor Concentration should be minor, unless your business is reliant exclusively upon one single supplier who is hard or impossible to replace.

A couple of other major factors to consider are product concentration and market concentration. If you sell only one product, or your products only appeal to a very specific market segment, then your business would be considered less valuable than a company successfully selling various products and appealing to a diverse market.

9.15 TECH DEBT

Tech Debt is the cost (or lost opportunity cost) a company incurs when updating, maintaining or implementing new technology or systems with a business. Too much Tech Debt can reduce a business' ability to be agile and create an inconsistent experience for its customers. Hence, Buyers will look to assess the amount of Tech Debt they will inherit as part of the acquisition. Capricious complexity, insufficient incremental change, and delayed improvements mean high maintenance costs and an increased risk of customer dissatisfaction – and therefore, a lower Multiplier.

Business owners often fail to understand the impact their Technology Stack has on their business Valuation. However, many aspects of the technology you use might significantly alter your company's value. While continuously adding more and more features to old products may seem like a short-term gain, it inevitably ends up being a *long-term pain*. Developers working on badly designed software often suffer the slings and arrows of never being able to write quality code, as they are constantly having to navigate buggy code. This can also lead to a more stressed engineering workforce that results in higher staff churn, affecting both costs and productivity when delivering features.

Tech Debt can also be a significant barrier to addressing pressing market needs and sustaining a competitive edge. Layers upon layers of technological architecture can hamper strategic imperatives for incumbent businesses, such as nimbleness and resilience, thus leaving them exposed to new entrants. Here are three points to consider when assessing your business' Tech Debt:

1. You should keep a gauge on your site's average technical downtime. If it's more than 5%, then this downtime is likely a recurring issue that will

require high maintenance costs in the future. In those cases, downtime should be addressed prior to selling if you wish to avoid creating Downward Pressure on your Multiplier.

2. Having a user-friendly backend will earn you big bonus points with Buyers. Generally, purchasers want to know that they are not acquiring a website that's a nightmare to maintain. If an individual can easily perform routine maintenance and navigate your site's primary functions without any technical expertise, potential Buyers will be more confident in a smooth transition.

3. Custom-built websites operating on unknown platforms increase the technical burden, especially for non-technical Buyers. Finding developers to work on proprietary software can be considerably more difficult and expensive. Contrarily, businesses operating on well-known, easy-to-operate Content Management System (CMS) platforms – such as Squarespace, Magento, WordPress, or Shopify – will be more attractive to Buyers, because they are cheaper, easier to update, and have more support resources. Since these popular platforms appeal to a broader audience, using them helps expand your potential Buyer pool. So unless you have an excellent reason to run your business on a custom-built website – with either a trusted in-house developer or a reliable freelancer under contract – evaluate a transition to a more popular platform at least six months before the sale.

It becomes obvious that reducing Tech Debt results in adding business Value. With the increased need for flexibility, adaptability, security, and Scalability in today's market, Tech Debt has moved beyond an IT matter to a broader business imperative that every Buyer will seek to address and evaluate. Buyers will look to determine whether or not the business can up its game in a timely manner in order to compete, grow, and prosper. Therefore, it is no surprise that increased Tech Dept can put downward pressure on the Multiplier, whereas businesses with moderate Tech Debt may see a slight boost on their Multiplier.

9.16 EXCLUDED ASSETS

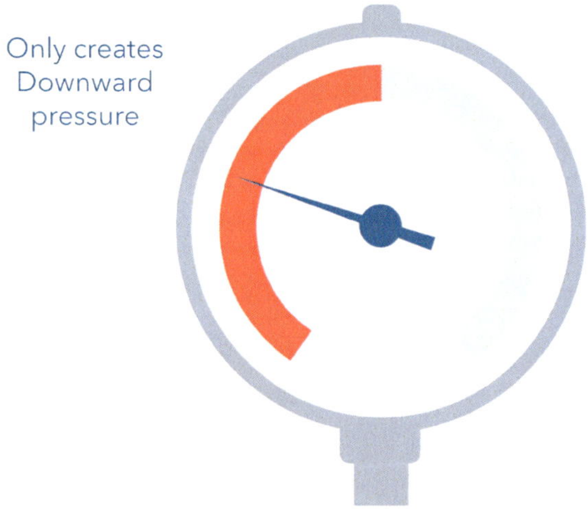

Which Assets are – or are not – included in the sale? Excluding Assets from the sale of your business tends to have a negative impact on Valuation and, in extreme cases, can render the business unsellable. The level of impact will depend on the perceived value of the excluded Assets and how the business would perform without them.

Excluding your laptop from the sale of your business is unlikely to have any impact on the value of your business. However, excluding customer data or a Facebook account almost certainly will. This is because you can determine the value of the laptop with a quick Google search and a little bit of common sense. But it is impossible to know the value of the Facebook account in relation to the business without monitoring how the business performs without it for six to 12 months. As you know well by now, uncertainty equals risk, and risk creates downward pressure on the Multiplier.

TIP: Prepare a full list of all Assets you are including in the sale – inventory, social media accounts, email lists, etc. – and be sure to highlight any Assets you do not plan on including in the sale. Review this list with your broker or advisor to learn how this may or may not impact the value of your business.

9.17 SALES STRUCTURE

Creates pressure in both directions

The way you structure the sale of your business will have a significant influence on your Valuation. This is because selling the corporate entity vs. solely its business Assets will have different tax implications for both you and the Buyer. Generally speaking, Buyers are willing to pay higher Multipliers for businesses selling Business Assets only and sellers are willing to accept lower Multipliers when selling the corporate entity. I'll explain why this is.

The relief business owners feel when selling their business after years of hard work can often be overshadowed by large and unexpected tax bills. That is why business owners must ensure that proper tax strategies are in place, in order to minimize tax penalties at the time of sale. In most jurisdictions, when you sell your business and generate income, you are liable for Capital Gains Tax (CGT).

Sellers are usually advised to seek Entrepreneurs' Relief for reducing the rate of CGT payable and explore forms of Rollover Relief (or Hold-over Relief) as a means of minimizing and deferring CGT Liability. How much tax you pay is mainly dependent on your company 's legal structure, where the business is based, and whether the sale is an Asset sale or a company stock sale.

On the Buyer's end, the pressures of tax Liability are of equal magnitude and importance. To maximize their tax position, Buyers will often conduct a pre-purchase tax evaluation to consider any tax relief strategies that would minimize repayments. Depending on the acquisition strategy, many Buyers might prefer to simply purchase the business' Assets rather than the legal corporate entity, in order to avoid fees and inherit the company's liabilities.

An entity sale, on the other hand, might be more advantageous for the seller, tax-wise and Liability-wise, but less so for the Buyer, who will be taking on the Liability risks of the corporate entity they are purchasing. Likewise, any stock purchase will attract additional taxes, for example Stamp Duty Land Tax (SDLT) if the purchase includes commercial real estate acquisition, and so on.

When structuring the purchase, Buyers and

sellers alike are advised to seek context-specific advice from a competent tax expert, in order to assess and quantify the real benefits of applicable tax-avoidance strategies. However, because tax Liability differs so much from jurisdiction to jurisdiction, we won't go into further specifics in this article, and it is highly recommended that you consult a qualified tax professional to limit your tax Liability prior to a sale.

Even though a Liability-free corporate entity might seek to sell the entire entity, an Asset sale may be more advantageous for both parties, as the value of each Asset class can be negotiated to serve common tax purposes.

9.18 SBA QUALIFIED

The Small Business Administration (SBA) loan program plays an important part in the financing of business acquisitions. Getting your business pre-qualified for an SBA loan is a great way to increase your business' value. If a Buyer can use an SBA loan to acquire your business, allowing them to debt finance their investment, doing so effectively lowers their capital requirements. This presents a huge bonus to Buyers, creating upward pressure on the Multiplier.

The SBA itself doesn't lend money, but they work closely with banks and lenders to provide entrepreneurs with solutions for obtaining financing. Although banks are generally eager to lend money on property purchases, business purchases are considered far riskier than real estate. Therefore, in order for a bank to lend money for a business purchase, the federal government has to mediate and guarantee the majority portion of the business loan through the SBA.

Apart from business acquisitions, SBA loans can also be used for other endeavors, such as purchase of equipment or company expansion. Any potential Buyer will appreciate having access to adequate funds for sustaining and growing the business they are buying, while minimizing risks and limitations of traditional financing methods. An SBA-backed loan provides the borrower with longer and better terms, as well as additional support and benefits of which they can avail.

However, since the Great Recession of 2008, the business brokerage community has witnessed a significant decrease in the number of approved SBA loans. Although banks are still willing to fund SBA loans, they usually add on many requirements for both sellers and buyers that were uncommon prior to 2008, some of which carry tax consequences for both parties.

The most popular type is the SBA 7(a) loan, and the requirements for its program serve as a base for most SBA loan prerequisites. In a general sense, qualifying for an SBA loan is feasible if you meet the following criteria:

- Operating a **for-profit business** – several exceptions and non-profit businesses are ineligible.

- Relevant requirements regarding the business' **headquarters location**.
- Meeting **small Business Size** requirements – generally, a business with less than 500 employees or between $750,000-$3,850,000 in annual revenue will qualify.
- **Credit score** requirements set by individual lenders, rather than the SBA. Most lenders require a personal credit score of at least 680 from all pre-eminent business owners and **clear credit history** regarding government debt.
- Again, most lenders are more likely to give a loan to **established businesses** with a minimum of two years of business operations and management experience in the industry. For startups, further requirements are in place regarding the business owner's ability to demonstrate **managerial experience** within the industry.
- A **sufficient debt-to-equity ratio** of 3x for new businesses, or 4x for established businesses is acceptable.
- A demonstrated **ability to repay the loan** with sufficient Cash Flow and a debt service coverage ratio (DSCR) of at least 1.25 to your business.
- SBA loans do not have to be fully collateralized, but obtaining financing is significantly easier with more personal and business **collateral**. Generally, you will be expected to provide an upfront payment of 10%-20% of the loan amount, in addition to backing the loan by pledging collateral.
- A **personal guarantee** required by the SBA from all who own 20% or more of the business, allowing the SBA and the lender to hold you personally accountable for the debt in case the business is unsuccessful. In such a case, along with the collateral mentioned above, your personal Assets can also be collected to secure the loan repayment.

Disclaimer: Please note that the above requirements may vary depending on your country and jurisdiction, and are subject to change.

At the end of the day, a business' value, no matter how high, will remain just a number on paper if no Buyer can obtain financing to purchase it. Therefore, the ease and availability with which SBA loans can be obtained by potential buyers can greatly affect your business' Valuation Multiplier.

Miscellaneous Drivers can have as much impact on the valuation and saleability of your online business as any other Value Pressure. Now that we've covered the most common drivers of online business value, it's time to put it all together.

ACTIVITY 9

Miscellaneous Pressure Gauges

1. Identify any Miscellaneous Pressures that you believe may apply Upward or Downward Pressure on your Valuation.

PRESSURE	↑ **Upward Pressure** ↓ **Downward Pressure**

2. Speak with an advisor or an experienced friend to determine how these Pressures may impact your valuation.

KEY TAKEAWAYS

MISCELLANEOUS PRESSURES

- In addition to the seven Value Pressures, there are 18 miscellaneous drivers that may also influence the current market value of your business.

- Market niche: Some niches are more sought after than others; greater demand usually creates upward pressure on the Earnings Multiplier.

- Recent changes: Change creates uncertainty around the future performance of your business, so avoid making changes for at least six months prior to selling to dodge any penalty to your Multiplier.

- Seasonality: Highly seasonal businesses usually sell for lower Multipliers than businesses with consistent year-round sales.

- Liability: Having a financial obligation to another entity that will result in cash outflow for prospective Buyers will negatively impact the Multiplier.

- Infringements: Infringing on another business' IP presents a significant risk to prospective Buyers, placing downward pressure on the Multiplier.

- Licensing: If the eventual acquirer needs a specific license to operate your business, it may reduce Buyer demand and therefore your Multiplier. It all depends on how common the license is and how easy it is to get licensed.

- Changing laws and market regulations: If your business is likely to be impacted (for better or worse) by upcoming market regulatory changes, Buyers will take this into consideration when valuing your business.

- Third-party compliance: Buyers will evaluate whether your business complies with partner and stakeholder terms and agreements as part of their due diligence. Any non-compliance represents risk, and will result in a lower Multiplier.

- Legal disputes: Commercial disputes (settled or ongoing) create unwanted risk, uncertainty and complexity for potential acquirers and usually place considerable downward pressure on the Multiplier.

- Non-competition: Your willingness to sign a three-to-five-year non-compete will have a significant bearing on the saleability and Valuation of your business.

- Exit Motivations: It is not uncommon for Buyers to grow weary of your motivations to sell your business. Any suspicion or uncertainty will result in a lower Earnings Multiplier, so be as honest and transparent as possible.

- Owner profile: Buyers will often run a background check on you as part of their due diligence process. If you have any skeletons in your closet, it is best to be upfront about it. If there is no information about you anywhere on the internet, it is worth investing some time into creating an online profile to build trust and credibility.

- Leadership and culture: Naturally, Buyers will pay more for a business with strong leadership and a positive, productive culture than one with zero leadership or a toxic culture.

- Concentration: If your most valuable customer represents more than 20% of sales, most Buyers will consider this to be a customer concentration risk. Similarly, a reliance on a single supplier or key partnership will also be considered risky business.

- Tech Debt: Tech Debt is the cost your business incurs when updating, maintaining or implementing new technology and systems. Too much Debt reduces a business' ability to be agile and can create an inconsistent customer experience. Hence why significant Tech Debt creates downward pressure on the Multiplier.

- Excluded Assets: Excluding Assets from the sale of your business tends to have a negative impact on Valuation and, in extreme cases, can render the business unsellable.

- Sales structure: The way you structure the sale of your business will have a significant influence on your Valuation. This is because selling the corporate entity vs. solely its business Assets will have different tax implications for both you and the Buyer.

- SBA Qualified: The Small Business Administration (SBA) loan program plays an important part in the financing of business acquisitions. Getting your business pre-qualified for an SBA loan is a great way to increase your business' value.

PUTTING IT ALL TOGETHER

10

10. PUTTING IT ALL TOGETHER

The aim of this book was to teach you three things:

1 How much your business is worth today.

You learned how to accurately calculate the value of your online business using the The Pressure Gauge Model™.

2 How to increase the value of your business.

You learned how The 8 Pressure Gauges influence your Valuation and how they can be manipulated to increase your net worth.

3 How to prepare your business for sale.

You went deep on Buyer psychology learning (i) how to remove obstacles in your business that might perturb them, and (ii) how to insert lures that make your business an attractive acquisition target.

We first got a solid understanding of how your business is likely to be valued in the market today. Next we calculated your Earnings. We then used comparative market data to establish your Base Multiplier before using the other seven Pressure Gauges to measure the Upward and Downward Pressure created on your Earnings Multiplier. Now all that's left is to calculate your earnings Multiplier to determine the current valuation of your business. Before we do, let's ground our learnings with one more short story.

JENNY'S LEMONADE ENTERPRISE

Remember Jenny's lemonade enterprise from Chapter 5? Let's use her story to reflect on all that we have learned in this book so far!

Due to COVID-19 Pandemic restrictions, Jenny's sales nose-dived and she decided that the juice was no longer worth the squeeze. She packed up her lemonade stall and went back to the drawing board. Before long, Jenny had sourced biodegradable bottles from Alibaba and was selling her bottled lemonade products through her Shopify store online. Over the past year, her business generated $230,000 in Revenue and $95,000 in Seller's Discretionary Earnings (SDE). Not a bad side-hustle for a nine year old.

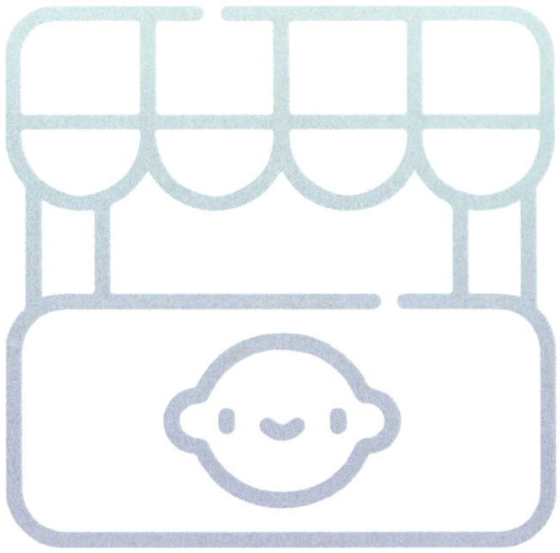

#1 BASE MULTIPLIER

So let's consider Jenny's Base Multiplier. We know that roughly 97 businesses out of 100 sell for a Multiplier between 0x and 5x. We also know that according to the best and most recent data available, the average sales Multiplier for eCommerce businesses is 2.96x. We know that the business is small and young, but it can't be too time-intensive because Jenny is in the third grade and hasn't skipped a single day of school. All considered, let's give Jenny's enterprise a starting base Multiplier of 2.84x.

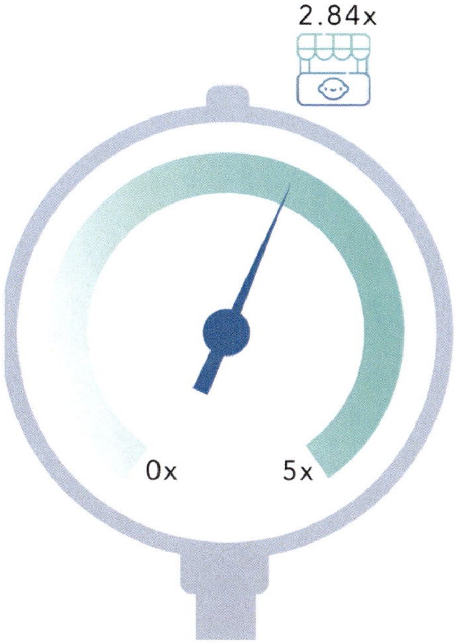

Base Multiplier: 2.84x
Valuation: $269,800

Key Influences
Business Model: eCommerce
Business Size: Small
Business Age: Young
Time Commitment: Moderate

#2: PERFORMANCE

Overall, Jenny's lemonade enterprise is performing well, with an impressive upward Trend in sales, a healthy rate of repeat customers, and a healthy ROI on customer acquisition spend. The strong performance creates Upward Pressure on the Multiplier, leading to a decent increase of +0.37x.

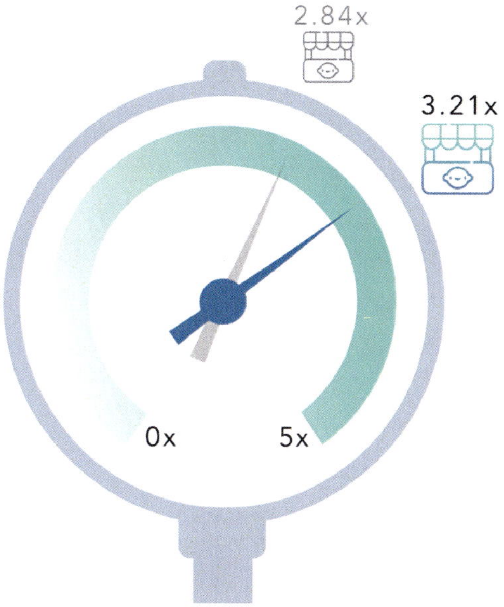

Multiplier Impact: +0.37
Adj. Multiplier: 3.21
Adj. Valuation: $304,950

Downward Pressure	Upward Pressure
Downward trend in average monthly User volume	Upward trend in sales Revenue
	High repeat customer rate %
	LTV:CAC Ratio = 6:1

#3 SUSTAINABILITY

Although Jenny's lemonade products are rated highly by customers and demand has been unaffected by the economic downturn, the business is heavily reliant on Facebook Ads. Brokers, valuers, and experienced Buyers are aware of the significant changes Facebook made to its newsfeed and algorithms in mid-to-late 2021, which casts uncertainty over the future performance of Jenny's Advertising ROI. As we know, uncertainty creates significant downward pressure on the Multiplier, resulting in a 0.55x reduction to Jenny's Multiplier.

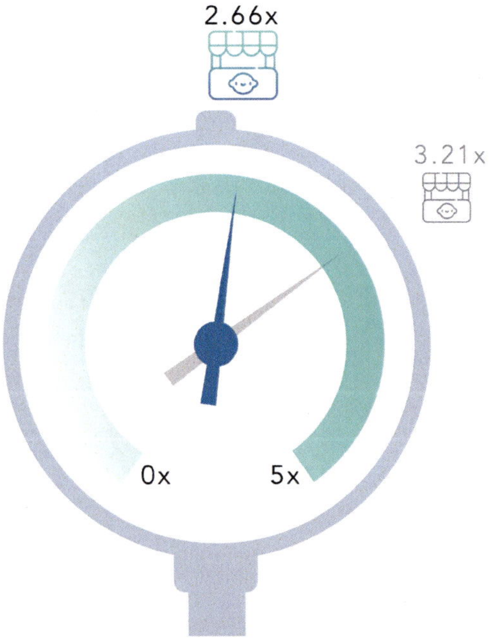

Multiplier Impact: -0.55
Adj. Multiplier: 2.66
Adj. Valuation: $252,700

Downward Pressure	Upward Pressure
Heavy reliance on single Traffic source (70% sales through Facebook ads)	4-star product rating Moderate to high Market Resilience

Action: Invest in email marketing and content / SEO to reduce dependency on Facebook ads.

#4 DEFENSIBILITY

As we know from Chapter 5, Jenny's customer base was unwaveringly loyal despite there being 10 new lemonade stands in her neighborhood by midsummer. These loyal customers continue to purchase from Jenny's online store today, accounting for the 30% of customers who aren't acquired through Facebook ads. Although Jenny cannot claim that her entire customer base is loyal to her brand, these local customers are serial repeat purchasers, representing significant Lifetime Value (LTV) to the business, which will likely win some minor bonus points (+0.11) with potential Buyers.

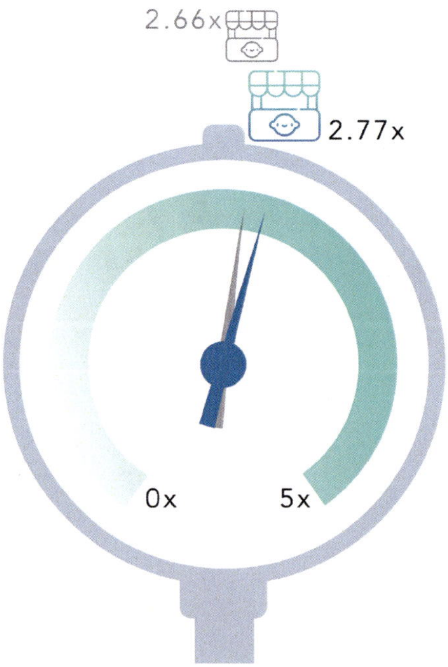

Multiplier Impact: +0.11
Adj. Multiplier: 2.77
Adj. Valuation: $263,150

Downward Pressure	Upward Pressure
N/A	Strong brand loyalty

#5 SCALABILITY

Jenny's business is no more or less scalable than the average owner-operated Physical Product eCommerce business. The business has not yet reached a point where it's experiencin Diminishing Rates of Return due to Market Saturation or Market Competition, so there is plenty of opportunity to scale her business. Jenny could increase the Scalability of her Business Model by introducing subscription-based pricing. She could also improve the Scalability of her operations by optimizing, automating and documenting business systems and processes. All considered, the Scalability of Jenny's business is unlikely to have any impact on current market value.

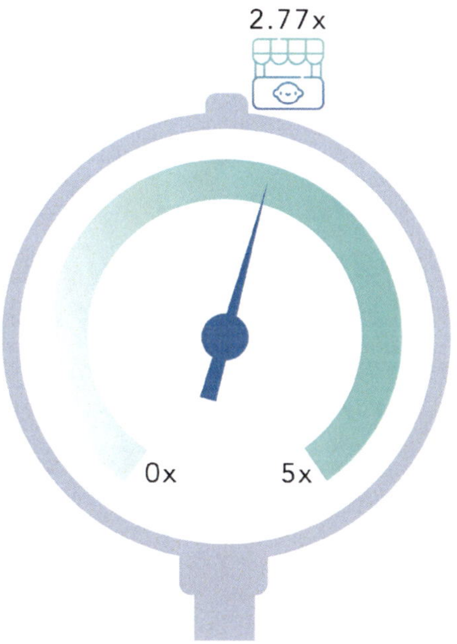

Multiplier Impact: +/- 0.00
Valuation: $262,150

Downward Pressure	Upward Pressure
N/A	N/A

#6 TRANSFERABILITY

Prospective Buyers will be understandably concerned about whether Jenny's high-value local customers will continue purchasing from the business if it's owned by someone other than Jenny. Afterall, these customers are Jenny's neighbors and they like to "*buy local*". If the prospective buyer is located over the other side of the country, or overseas, it is possible that a fair chunk of these customers may stop shopping with the online lemonade store.

Although the lack of Transferability has placed downward pressure on the Multiplier, there are also a number of other areas of the business where Jenny can significantly improve its Transferability. These include completing administrative tasks such as creating an SOP document, getting written agreements in place with key partners and stakeholders, or switching out her personal Paypal account for a Business PayPal account. She may even consider hiring a part-time staff member to replace her father, who is currently acting as her Customer Support Manager and Finance/Admin Officer.

Alas, as of today, prospective buyers have reasonable cause for concern as to whether or not a portion of the repeat / serial customer base will

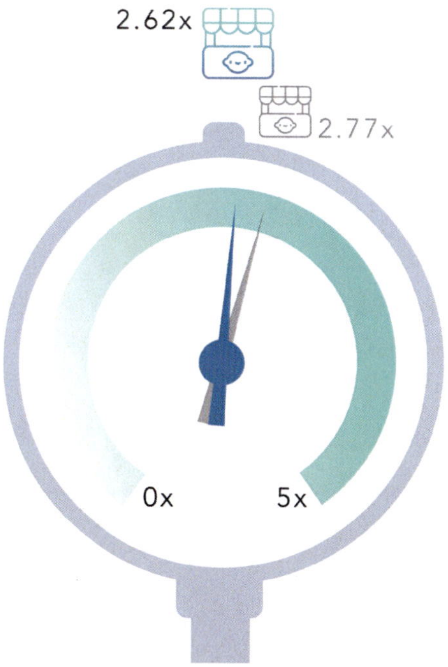

continue to purchase from new ownership or not. Until Jenny addresses this issue, it's likely to hurt her Multiplier Score.

Multiplier Impact: -0.15
Adj. Multiplier: 2.62
Adj. Valuation: $248,900

Downward Pressure	Upward Pressure
Customer loyalty tied to owner	Low degree of specialized knowledge required to run the business
No SOP or documented procedures of any kind	
Personal PayPal account is not transferable	
Part-time staff (Jenny's Dad) will not continue under new ownership.	
No written agreement in place with key partners and stakeholders	

Actions:

- Create SOP document
- Create PayPal business and migrate customers across
- Hire and train a part-time teammate to take over some responsibilities from Jenny and her Dad.
- Secure written agreements with key stakeholders

#7 AUDITABILITY

Despite having lots of financial data, Traffic data and customer data, Jenny will need to stop using her business bank account for personal expenses and draft up some operational procedure documents to avoid any adverse impact on her business' Multiplier. As it stands today, potential Buyers cannot determine with any real confidence whether there are any undisclosed business expenses, or whether Jenny's claim of spending only 10 hours a week running the business is entirely accurate. Therefore, Jenny can expect the Multiplier to dip some more.

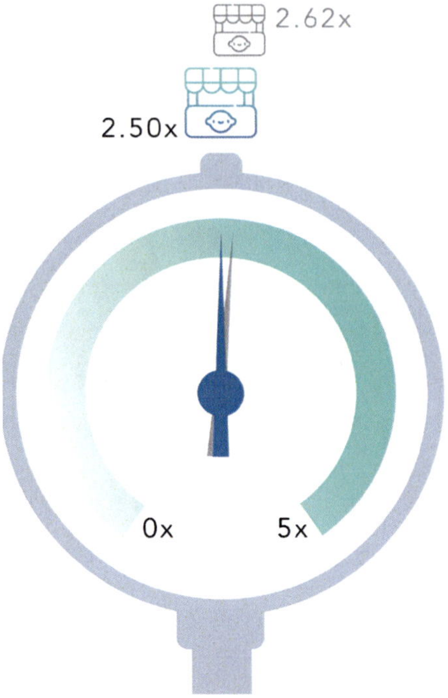

Multiplier Impact: -0.12
Adj. Multiplier: 2.50
Adj. Valuation: $237,500

Downward Pressure	Upward Pressure
Commingled accounts	Google Analytics data
No SOP or documented procedures of any kind	Shopify customer data Metrics
	Profit & loss statement
	Tax return

Actions:

- Create a separate bank account for business-related transactions only.
- Create SOP document

#8 MISCELLANEOUS VALUE PRESSURES

No miscellaneous Value Pressures had any significant impact on the value of Jenny's business. However, if she were able to get her business pre-approved for an SBA loan in the future, she could look to improve the value and saleability of her business by a considerable margin.

So Jenny's Valuation started at $269,800, went as high as $304,950, and finally landed at $237,500. If Jenny checks off the seven items on her Exit Plan Checklist below, she can easily expect to make an extra $75,000 on her exit payday - and that's being conservative. In all likelihood, a number of these exit plan initiatives will lead to more sales and higher Earnings increasing her valuation further.

So Jenny's Valuation started at $269,800, went as high as $304,950, and finally landed at $237,500. If Jenny checks off the seven items on her Exit Plan Checklist below, she can easily expect to make an extra $75,000 on her exit payday - and that's being conservative. In all likelihood, a number of these exit plan initiatives will lead to more sales and higher Earnings increasing her valuation further.

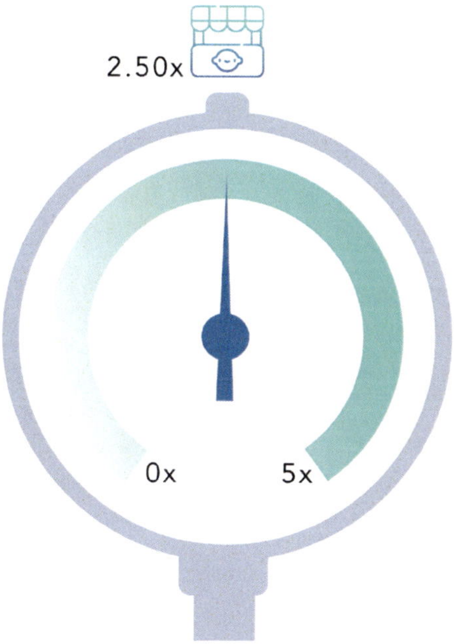

Multiplier Impact: +/- 0.00
Adj. Multiplier: 2.50
Valuation: $237,500

Downward Pressure	Upward Pressure
N/A	N/A

JENNY'S EXIT PLAN CHECKLIST

- ✓ Diversify Customer Channels - invest in newsletter marketing and SEO.
- ✓ Develop an SOP manual
- ✓ Get a written stakeholder agreements in place that continues under new ownership
- ✓ Switch out personal PayPal account for Business PayPal Account
- ✓ Contract a part-time customer support/ admin worker.
- ✓ Detangle commingled bank account and stop running personal transactions through the account
- ✓ Get business SBA pre-approved

ACTIVITY 10

Putting it all together

1. Calculate your Multiplier

____

2. Create your own Exit Plan Checklist

☐ ______________________________

☐ ______________________________

☐ ______________________________

☐ ______________________________

☐ ______________________________

☐ ______________________________

☐ ______________________________

☐ ______________________________

GLOSSARY

Add-Backs: The broad term refers to business Expenses which, while part of the operating costs, are not critical for generating core revenue, and therefore evaluators mostly seek to exclude these items from the estimated value.

Advertising ROI: The amount of profit generated from ads and free product listings, versus the amount spent on those ads.

Asset: A resource of value that belongs to and helps run your business.

Audience Growth Rate: This metric measures how fast your brand's followers, and therefore exposure, are increasing on social media.

Audit: Examination of a company's financial data, as well as any other relevant data, to verify whether or not the business' value claims are correct.

Auditability: Measured by a Buyer's ability to verify everything you claim about your business.

Average Dwell Time: The time a User spends on evaluating if your content will provide the information they need after clicking on your page from the Google search results.

Average Purchase Frequency: The average number of purchases a customer makes over the course of a predefined period.

Average Time On Page: How much time a visitor spends on your webpage or post.

Average Revenue Per User: ARPU or average revenue per unit, is a company's total revenue, divided by its number of subscribers.

Base Multiplier: The starting point from which Buyers, brokers, and independent valuers all begin their Valuation, determined through a process of benchmarking a handful of online business statistics (Business Model, Age, Size, Owner Time Commitment).

Bootstrapper: Someone who relies on their own resources to start and scale their business.

Break-Even: Often abbreviated as B/E, is where a Buyer reaches a point where the business they acquired has generated enough Earnings to recuperate the cost of their initial spend, i.e. the acquisition cost.

Business Model: Specifically relates to the different ways in which a business is monetized.

Business Size: The scale or volume of a company's operations.

Cash Flow: The amount of money a business has generated or consumed over a defined period.

Channel Diversity: Relates to the mix of channels used to acquire new customers. A business that relies too heavily on a single Customer Channel is usually considered a lot riskier than a business acquiring customers through multiple channels.

Churn Rate: The percentage of customers who stop buying from you.

Consumable Trap: The trap created by some companies that lock their customers by being the exclusive provider of the consumables for their base product, like Hewlett-Packard with the cartridges for their printers.

Content Marketing: The creation, distribution, and publishing of content for a targeted online audience. This content may not explicitly promote your brand, but the intent is to stimulate your audience's interest in your product or services by using well-organized content strategies.

Content Marketing ROI: The effectiveness of your Content Marketing strategy in generating a profit will be ultimately determined by your Content Marketing ROI.

Conversion: When a consumer of a marketing message performs a certain action that's a part of a marketing funnel or campaign.

Conversion Rate: The best way to measure the financial performance of your advertising campaigns, and the main reason you invested in them in the first place.

Cost Advantage: Achieved when one company purchases in mass quantities to achieve a lower price per unit than competitors.

Cost of goods sold (CoGS): The direct costs incurred by producing the goods that a company sells.

Cost Per Acquisition (CPA): This Metric measures the total cost advertisers pay to acquire one paying customer.

Cost-Per-Click (CPC): An alternative to CPM, this Metric that platforms such as Google AdWords and Facebook use to bill in Pay-Per-Click (PPC) marketing campaigns, based on how many times an advertisement is clicked.

Cost-Per-Thousand Impressions (CPM): This Metric is the most common method for pricing web ads in digital marketing, and refers to the price based on every 1,000 times your ad appears before a User.

Clickthrough Rate: This Metric is used to determine the success of an email campaign, by measuring the percentage of email recipients who clicked on the links included in a given email.

Customer (Acquisition) Channel: The different platforms on which a customer engages with your brand, via your website, your social media platforms, and even email.

Customer Acquisition Cost: Amount it costs to win a customer to purchase your product or service.

Customer Funnel: The incremental steps that a prospective customer takes on their path to conversion.

Customer Lifetime Value: Measures the net value of a customer.

Customer Relationship Management (CRM): The technologies, strategies, and processes that a brand uses to track, manage, and analyze interactions with customers, and the resulting data.

Customer Retention: A business' ability to retain its customers over time. This Metric not only measures the percentage of retained customers by the end of a given time period, but also indicates how successful a business is at satisfying its existing customers.

Customer Retention Rate: The ratio of customers that continue to buy from you throughout your business' lifecycle.

Customer Review: A review by a customer of a given business on a particular product or service they've purchased and experienced.

Customer Value: The worth of a particular product or service to a customer, compared to the alternatives available.

Data Migration: The process of selecting, preparing, extracting, and transforming data and permanently transferring it from one computer storage system to another.

Data Trap: The catch customers find themselves in when their customer data is only available on a particular channel, and cannot be migrated to another app.

Defensibility: A company's ability to defend market share.

Defense Barriers: Also known as *Barriers to Entry*, these are tactics a business can use to increase its ability to defend its market share.

Diminishing Rates of Return: When a business reaches a point where the Customer Acquisition Cost starts to increase.

Direct traffic: Website traffic that doesn't come from a referring website.

Display Advertising Traffic: Website traffic acquired through display ad networks, such as AdWords, AdRoll, etc.

Domain Authority (DA): Measures how strong, authoritative, or 'famous' your website is compared to other sites.

Downward Pressure: Occurs when a certain business element or characteristic reduces the Earnings Multiplier and therefore value of a Business.

Earnings: Net benefits produced by a company's operations, and is often also the amount on which an entity must pay corporate tax.

Email Traffic: The number of visitors driven to a website through email marketing campaign CTAs.

Equity: The amount (in percentage form) of shares owned by an entity or person in a particular company.

Grandfather Pricing: A term for pricing where customers continue paying the same price for a product or service despite a business' price increases for its newer customers.

Google Analytics: (GA) is widely considered to be the most comprehensive web Traffic analytics platform.

Investor: A person or entity who commits capital to improve or grow a product or service, with the expectation of gaining financial returns later on.

Learning Curve Trap: The time and expense of learning, configuring, and customizing a new product/device/software creates a significant learning curve, which can trap business operators into a huge time investment.

Lengthy Cancellation Process: Service providers usually incorporate a complex and Lengthy Cancellation Process with significant waiting time and paperwork involved.

Liability: A business' financial obligation to another entity arising from its implication in past events or transactions.

Lifetime Value: (LTV) measures the gross value of a customer.

Link Profile: The makeup of external links, known as backlinks, that a company's website domain receives from other websites, either for citing a reference from a website's content or backing up facts and statistics.

List Growth Rate: This metric describes the rate at which a business' email list is growing.

Lowest Price: An old-school technique typically used by larger companies to kill off competition by offering products and services at prices where competitors and new entrants struggle to make a Profit.

Market Competition: If your business operates in a larger market, you might find yourself bumping your head on the same glass ceiling but for another reason entirely - *competition*. Big markets usually have big players, and big players are often bullies.

Market Saturation: If your business operates in a small market, you may find yourself bumping your head on a glass ceiling, where growth becomes difficult due to Market Saturation. This is particularly common in highly niche-specific markets.

Market Resilience: A business' ability to sustain performance during economic downturns, market disruptions, and other adversities.

Merchant: A person who buys and sells goods produced by others.

Metrics: Measurements of key quantitative data that companies use to compare, track, and analyze business performance.

Multiplier: The number by which a business' value can be multiplied to determine its actual value, which is calculated by considering all aspects of a business.

Net Promoter Score (NPS): This Metric measures customer satisfaction and loyalty by asking customers the likelihood of them recommending the company/product/service in question to friends, relatives, and colleagues on a scale from 1 to 10.

Network Economies: Achieved when you reach a tipping point where each new customer you acquire improves the experience for all of your customers.

Organic Search Traffic: Website traffic generated when people click on your organic listing on search engines such as Google and Bing.

Organic Traffic Value: Estimated amount of money you would be paying for Traffic from all the keywords your website is ranking for if you pay via Google's Pay-Per-Click (PPC) instead of trying to rank for them organically.

Owner Drawings: A withdrawal of funds by a business owner from the business' resources, for personal use.

Owner Time Commitment: Amount of time an owner dedicates to working on his business during a normal week.

Page Depth: Average number of your website's pages that Users visit after your landing page.

Pages Per Session: Average number of pages visited by your Users during a session. Basically, it shows you how 'sticky' your site is, so naturally, you should be aiming for a high number.

Paid Search: Also known as PPC, it is where you pay to appear on the first page of a search engine's search results for certain keywords.

Paid Search Traffic: Traffic that comes to your website via a paid advertisement or sponsored listing on a given search engine.

Paid traffic: Any customer who visits your website via a paid advertising promotion.

Pay-Per-Click: Type of marketing that allows businesses to leverage search engine advertising to generate clicks to their website, as opposed to "earning" those same clicks organically.

Potential Reach: A business' Potential Reach measures the number of people who could potentially and realistically view your post during a reporting period.

Post Reach: The dissemination of your content and the size of the audience that views it.

Pressure: Occurs when a certain business element

or characteristic increases or decreases the value of a Business.

Purchase Frequency: Average number of purchases a customer makes within a given time period from a particular seller.

Referral Traffic: Website traffic generated from a link that appears on another site.

Refund Rate: Percentage of transactions that are returned to the client.

Retention Time Period: Amount of time a customer remains loyal to a given brand.

Scalability: Ability by which a company can grow its Revenue while maintaining or reducing its cost base.

Search Marketing: Incorporation of SEO tactics in online content and site architecture in order to increase a website's visibility and achieve a higher ranking in SERPs.

Search Ranking: Position a company's website holds in the search results for a specific search query.

Seller feedback: Like a report card from your customers, indicating the quality of the customer experience you provide.

Social Media Traffic: Website visitors acquired through social platforms such as Facebook, Instagram, Twitter, Youtube, and LinkedIn.

Social Share of Voice (SSoV): The market share equivalent of the social media world.

Sustainability: A measurement of the likelihood of sustaining current business performance in the future.

Switching Costs: The time, resources, money and mental effort required from a customer to switch your product or service out for an alternative.

Technology Stack: All the different technology services required to build and run a single application.

Termination Fee: The money paid when one party wants to terminate the term of an agreement or long-term contract.

Third-Party Platform: A platform that a business doesn't own, but does business with (such as a social media platform like Facebook).

Traffic: The flow of data across the internet as a whole, or within certain network links of the whole.

Trend: The general direction of change or developments within popular culture.

Unsubscribe Rate: The percentage of Users who have opted-out from your mailing list.

Upward Pressure: Occurs when a certain business element or characteristic increases the Earnings Multiplier and therefore value of a Business.

Users: Anyone who interacts with your business through your website.

Valuation: An accurate measure of what the highest bidder in the market is willing to pay for a business.

Value Pressures: Are the primary mechanisms that make up your business' value, creating Upward Pressure or Downward Pressure on the Earnings Multiplier and value of a Business.

Virality Rate: The amount of people who shared your post in proportion to its number of Impressions (Unique Views) during a specific period.Value Pressures: Are the primary mechanisms that make up your business' value, creating Upward Pressure or Downward Pressure on the Earnings Multiplier and value of a Business.

Virality Rate: Virality Rate refers to the amount of people who shared your post in proportion to its number of Impressions (Unique Views) during a specific period.

ABOUT THE AUTHOR

Jamie Toyne is the Founder and former CEO of Dealflow Brokerage. He now runs a business accelerator program called DKAccelerator and has his own business coaching and consulting practice (jamietoyne.com). Jamie grew up in the small town of Mparntwe (Alice Springs) in the Central Deserts of Australia. He moved to Melbourne to complete a degree in Business Entrepreneurship at RMIT before interning at a tech start-up called Flippa.com, where he eventually became the Director of Brokerage and was responsible for scaling Flippa's business brokerage division in San Francisco, California. Over the past decade Jamie has helped hundreds of entrepreneurs successfully exit their businesses. After living in Puerto Escondido, Mexico, for two years, where he became addicted to surfing, he has returned home to Mparntwe to give back to the community that raised him. Between running DKAccelerator and his coaching and consulting practice, Jamie creates educational content like this guide to support entrepreneurs on their journey.

Made in United States
Orlando, FL
04 November 2026

90201569R00102